managing yourself

DO THIS –
LIFE GETS

AND YOUR
BETTER

managing yourself

coach yourself to optimum emotional intelligence

Paul Morgan

www.yourmomentum.com
the stuff that drives you

momentum

What is momentum?

Momentum is a completely new publishing philosophy, in print and online, dedicated to giving you more of the information, inspiration and drive to enhance who you are, what you do, and how you do it.

Fusing the changing forces of work, life and technology, momentum will give you the bright stuff for a brighter future and set you on the way to being all you can be.

Who needs momentum?

Momentum is for people who want to make things happen in their career and their life, who want to work at something they enjoy and that's worthy of their talent and their time.

Momentum people have values and principles, and question who they are, what they do, and who for. Wherever they work, they want to feel proud of what they do. And they are hungry for information, stimulation, ideas and answers …

Momentum online

Visit *www.yourmomentum.com* to be part of the talent community. Here you'll find a full listing of current and future books, an archive of articles by momentum authors, sample chapters and self-assessment tools. While you're there, post your worklife questions to our momentum coaches and sign up to receive free newsletters with even more stuff to drive you.

More momentum

If you need more drive for your life, try one of these other momentum titles:

soultrader
personal career strategies for life
Carmel McConnell

reinvent yourself
tactics for work, life and happiness – yours
J. Jonathan Gabay

mental space
how to find clarity in a complex life
Tina Konstant and Morris Taylor

be your own career consultant
work out where you want to be – and get there
Gary Pyke and Stuart Neath

managing brand me
how to build your personal brand
Thomas Gad and
Anette Rosencreutz

coach yourself
make real change in your life
Anthony M. Grant and Jane Greene

change activist
make big things happen fast
Carmel McConnell

lead yourself
be where others will follow
Mick Cope

happy mondays
putting the pleasure back into work
Richard Reeves

the big difference
life works when you choose it
Nicola Phillips

hey you!
pitch to win in an ideas economy
Will Murray

snap, crackle or stop
change your career and create your own
destiny
Barbara Quinn

float you
how to capitalize on your talent
Carmel McConnell and Mick Cope

from here to e
equip yourself for a career in the wired
economy
Lisa Khoo

grow your personal capital
what you know, who you know and how you
use it
Hilarie Owen

clued up
working through politics and complexity
Alan Robertson and Graham Abbey

free agent manual
the rules and tools for your solo success
Josephine Monroe

PEARSON EDUCATION LIMITED

Head Office:
Edinburgh Gate
Harlow CM20 2JE
Tel: +44 (0)1279 623623
Fax: +44 (0)1279 431059

London Office:
128 Long Acre, London WC2E 9AN
Tel: +44 (0)20 7447 2000
Fax: +44 (0)20 7447 2170
Website: www.yourmomentum.com
        www.business-minds.com

First published in Great Britain in 2003

ISBN 1843 04023 9

British Library Cataloguing in Publication Data
A CIP catalogue record for this book can be
obtained from the British Library.

10 9 8 7 6 5 4 3 2 1

Typeset by Northern Phototypesetting Co. Ltd,
Bolton
Printed and bound in Great Britain by
Henry Ling Ltd, Dorchester

Cover design by Heat
Text design by Claire Brodmann Book Designs,
Lichfield, Staffs

*The Publishers' policy is to use paper
manufactured from sustainable forests.*

thank you…

Thanks to Neil Moult at Vision2learn.com and Rachael Stock at momentum for having faith in my Emotional Intelligence expertise.

I would like to dedicate this book to Marie and Natasha.

chapter one
my promise to you

chapter two
old maps and empty rooms

chapter three
self-awareness – it's a wonderful life

chapter four
goal setting – step forward
Julie Andrews

chapter five
empathy – knowing you

chapter six
intuition – magical feelings

chapter seven
integrity: you can't fake it

chapter eight
creativity – catching monkeys and empty car parks

chapter nine
emotional management –
marshmallows and mental toughness

chapter ten
just do it!

chapter one
my promise to you

Are you the sort of person who should read this book?

I was tempted to omit this section. Or hide it away in the text. Surely it would be better to have you buy the book and then work out whether it is of any use to you. That way I get my royalties whatever the result! However, on reflection, I would be happier for the casual browser to look through this section and then make their buy/don't buy decision. I would like those people who read through the checklist and decide they don't need the book to get in touch with me – if you are one of these you are a very rare species. Take a look at the checklist below now.

Checklist

Read through the questions below. If you answer no to any of the questions then the techniques in this book can help you.

- Do you have a detailed knowledge of how your beliefs, thoughts and feelings influence the results you get in life?
- Do you have a high level of self-awareness of how you think and feel and how life events influence your thoughts and feelings?
- Do you have a clearly defined personal vocation?
- Do you know how to set goals in ways that maximize your results?
- Are you adept at reading the emotional responses of other people?
- Do you know how to access and use your intuitions?
- Are you able to build trusting relationships?

- Are you readily able to come up with creative ideas that work?

- Are you able to easily tap into the emotional response that maximizes your results?

- Are you mentally resilient when put under pressure?

If you have answered no at any time then this book is for you. It is packed full of techniques that will show you a lot about yourself that you probably didn't know and that will help you to develop a whole range of skills and attributes that could really change your life. You'll develop self-awareness and uncover how much you are doing 'on automatic' without knowing you do it. You'll be helped to find your true vocation in life. You will also learn how to tap into your natural intuitions and creativity. You'll learn how to 'read' other people and how to build high-quality, trusting relationships. You will learn how to manage your emotions so that you are happier and more successful.

This book will also give you the tools and techniques to make changes if you want to do so. It may sound, to you, like just another self-help book. So, what's the difference between this book and others you may have read?

How this book differs from traditional self-help books

This book is about managing your most vital asset: you. It will focus upon helping you to improve the quality of your life. The smart reader will already have, rightly, concluded that this is a personal development book. I want it to be different from the traditional self-help books, so here I am making three promises to you, the reader:

1   You will not be subjected to my autobiographical rags to riches story.

2   You will not be asked to hug trees or speak to your guardian angel.

3   You will not be promised that each technique in this book works perfectly every time.

Rags to riches

'I once was lost and now am found.'

Lyric from 'Amazing Grace'

I have read a few personal development books in my time. Often a large portion of the book is dedicated to the author's life story. Invariably, they start out as a 'loser'. They were bankrupt, addicted to something or in broken relationships – or often all three. They were at rock bottom. Then they learned about the 'method'. This is some approach or technique that completely turned their life around. Now the personal development guru is living a wonderful life. Everything in the garden is rosy. And it is all due to the 'method' that you can now buy in seminar, audio, video or book format.

The guru has gone from zero to hero. They have become rich by telling others how they became rich. By doing this, they have painted themselves into a corner. If they admit to any difficulties in their life then their method and their business and their whole livelihood is threatened. Fortunately, they all appear to have perfect lives!

Sadly, for the purposes of this book, I do not have a heart wrenching story. I have never been in rags. A few problems here and there but rags, no. Nor have I become a mega-millionaire by selling a few easy-to-use techniques. However, I know that my experience and the experiences of hundreds of thousands of other people show that it is possible to make quick, permanent and positive changes in your life.

Hugging trees

One of the most popular approaches to personal development arises from the study of ancient cultures and religions. Or from the religious experience of a charismatic leader. There are thousands of these to be found in book or seminar form. You may end up hugging a tree. You may get in touch with your inner child or your guardian angel (possibly both). Elsewhere, you may get the chance to relive your birth. All these methods and more may be enjoyable. They may work but they will not be addressed in this book.

The bulk of the approaches described above have not been tested rigorously. Nor proven scientifically. There has not been a systematic review of the claims being made for these approaches. In contrast, the outstanding research that underpins what is found in this book has been done in real-life contexts. It has measurably improved the lives of tens of thousands of people. When 'alternative' approaches prove themselves in a similar way, their ideas will be found in this book.

During the previous 10 years, this detailed research has been brought together under the heading of 'Emotional Intelligence'. This term will be explained further later in this chapter. What is abundantly clear is that there are behaviours, competencies, and skills that can be called emotional intelligence (EI). It has been scientifically proven that a higher EI is linked to a better quality of life. Most important, it is abundantly clear that EI is not fixed. You can increase it and reap the benefits. This is not an act of faith – like alternative methods are. It is an act of fact.

Perfect methods

'I am not perfect but parts of me are excellent.'

Ashleigh Brilliant

Let me be absolutely unequivocal about one thing: The techniques in this book work perfectly – except when they do not. I won't sit on the fence on this issue.

The notion that the formulaic use of half a dozen techniques will always transform your life is nonsense. It is a dangerous nonsense. Every person is unique. They have a unique genetic structure (identical twins excluded), unique environments and have a variety of situations in which they live. To suggest that a one-size-fits-all method is a cure all is a little . . . iffy.

The notion that the formulaic use of half a dozen techniques will always transform your life is nonsense.

One of the less attractive outcomes of this perfect approach is the way its users may be treated if positive results are not forthcoming. One common response is to blame the user – they obviously did not apply the techniques correctly. When this happens the user has failed to understand something. Few personal development gurus will question their own powers of explanation! Alternatively, the user is said to have been undisciplined in their use of the technique. The implication is always clear; the master used it diligently and succeeded, which means you can too. If the expert can go from rags to riches then so can you. For the gurus a poor result by a user means they must either question their techniques or the user. No contest!

In this book you will be given dozens of proven techniques for improving your life. The challenge for you is to try them out and find what works. Yes, you will have to be thorough and disciplined. In all likelihood the exercises and techniques will help you to improve your life. Some will work very quickly. However, should you find that some techniques do not work for you, do not worry. If you have really tried something out there is probably a very good reason for your lack of progress: the technique is not for you. There does not need to be blame or guilt or any sense of failure. Simply conclude that, at this point in time, the technique was not for you. Then move on and use something else. Take a look at other techniques in this book, look elsewhere and speak to other interested people. Do so until you find something that works for you. There is a simple four step process for using any life-improvement techniques:

1 Ensure you are using the technique as prescribed.

2 Be willing to experiment with your improvised variations if step 1 does not work.

3 Be confident that you 'gave it a go'.

4 If steps 1–3 still do not bring the desired results, you should conclude that the technique is not for you. Find something else that will work.

When an approach to personal development relies on a few techniques then it can ill afford to disregard them. There will be many techniques provided in later chapters. Your mission – if you choose to take it – is to apply the techniques and find out which ones work for you.

A lot is known about the personal qualities that cause a person to have a better quality of life. They are covered in the introductory checklist (see page 2). These qualities can be managed by you. Once you spot any personal weaknesses you can take action and make positive changes. All these qualities – such as goal setting, intuition, creativity and resilience – have been studied for decades by psychologists. In recent years the many strands of diverse research have been drawn together and it is collectively referred to as Emotional Intelligence. So let's take a closer look at this concept.

What is emotional intelligence?

If you are going to manage yourself successfully then you need to understand the psychological ideas that underpin Emotional Intelligence (EI). These ideas offer all of us the opportunity to take control of our lives and significantly improve their quality.

IQ and other models

For over a hundred years psychologists have defined, measured and used the concept of the Intelligence Quotient (IQ). Such was their success that IQ became the one and only way to define what makes a person intelligent. The key intellectual elements of IQ were:

◆ linguistic skills

◆ analytical skills

◆ spatial orientation

◆ logical reasoning.

While this approach continued to be influential, it was challenged. It was obvious that many gifted and talented people did not necessarily score well in IQ tests. This did not seem to make sense. From the 1970s onwards, new approaches emerged. A highly influential model came from the research of Howard Gardener, a professor of psychology at Harvard. He developed the idea of multiple intelligences (MI). In his definitions there were seven categories:

1 Linguistic – talent with language

2 Mathematical/Logical – talent with maths/logic/systems

3 Visual/Spatial – visual talent

4 Musical – talent with music

5 Bodily/Physical – talent with movement and co-ordination

6 Interpersonal – social talent

7 Intrapersonal – talent for inner control and understanding.

The multiple intelligence approach makes a lot more sense to the layperson. There are athletes and dancers with phenomenal physical intelligence who may not be good at mathematical reasoning. Likewise, there are gifted musicians or those people who have great interpersonal skills who may not score well on a traditional IQ test. When you take a look around at many of life's achievers, they may not have the highest IQ. However, they are very likely to score highly in one or more of the multiple intelligences.

In 1990, Dr Peter Salovey and Dr John Mayer published two articles on the subject of emotional qualities and capabilities. They provided the first formal definition of emotional intelligence and provide the first demonstration that certain ability tasks could be used to measure this concept.

'Emotional Intelligence involves: the ability to perceive accurately, appraise and express emotions; the ability to access and/or generate feeling when they facilitate thought; the ability to understand emotion and emotional knowledge; and the ability to regulate emotions to promote emotional and intellectual growth.' Mayer & Salovey (1997)

It was in 1995 that most people became aware of EI. This was due to the best-selling book by Dr Daniel Goleman, *Emotional Intelligence: Why it can matter more than IQ*. In this book, Goleman presented a detailed account of cutting edge research, some of it based on studies that had run for decades. It showed that people with higher emotional intelligence were healthier and happier.

Reuven Bar-On is the Funding Director of the Institute of Applied Intelligence. He has been a central figure in the defining, measuring and applying of EI since 1980. He coined the term 'EQ' and created the first test of emotional intelligence.

Approaches to clustering emotional intelligences

There are many active researchers and writers on this subject. They cluster EI abilities in a number of ways (see below).

Salovey and Mayer

◆ identifying emotions

◆ using emotions

◆ understanding emotions

◆ managing emotions

Goleman

◆ self-awareness

◆ self-management

◆ social awareness

◆ social skills

Bar-On

◆ intrapersonal skills

◆ interpersonal skills

◆ adaptability

◆ stress management

◆ general mood

We do not need to concern ourselves with the schisms and conflicts in the world of EI. What is evident from all the research, however, is that a higher EI is strongly correlated with a higher quality of life, and that it is possible to raise EI levels through training. This final point is crucially important. We can improve our emotional intelligence and improve our lives.

We can improve our emotional intelligence and improve our lives.

The research shows that EI competencies and skills make a difference in business performance. David McClelland (1998) reviewed 30 companies and found that higher EI scores differentiated the top performers from average ones. Likewise, Boyatzis (1999) showed that distinguishing factors among high-level leaders were EI competencies. He found that these competencies raised incremental profits in the financial services sector by 78 per cent up to a staggering 390 per cent. A piece of research by Spencer and Spencer (1993) looked at high-performing individuals in health and social services, technical, sales, customer management, leadership and executive roles. Once again, EI proved to be a key factor. Here are some of their findings.

◆ Centre for Creative Leadership identified that low EI was most likely to cause career problems for senior executives.

◆ USA National Insurance company found that high EI staff outperformed low EI staff by over 100 per cent.

◆ University of Manchester Institute of Science and Technology found that high EI managers were healthier, happier and performed better than others. They also reported that managers can be taught to increase their EI.

◆ A study of 500 organizations indicated that those high on EI rise to the top.

◆ Qualities such as emotional self-awareness, empathy and problem solving are better predictors of sales success background or sales techniques.

◆ Physicians in the USA who were low on empathy were more likely to be sued.

One psychologist who has had a significant influence on emotional intelligence research is Professor Martin Seligman. He has done groundbreaking work on explanatory styles and learned optimism. In his book *What you can change and what you can't*, he clearly delineates between those aspects of our lives that we can change and those we cannot. Fortunately, the characteristics that make up EI are in the changeable category. Furthermore many of the changes can be achieved quickly with easy to use techniques.

The remainder of this book will focus on those factors that can improve the quality of your life. Those factors that can be changed. It will provide ways of making changes as quickly and effectively as possible.

'In the choice between changing one's mind and proving there's no need to do so, most people get busy on the proof.'

J. K. Galbraith

About the book

In the next chapter you will be given some useful models on how you think and how you make changes. You will be encouraged to take on the challenges of making personal changes. You will be encouraged to manage yourself more effectively. This way you can improve the results that you get in life.

The information in chapters 3–9 will be structured in an easy to follow format. First you will be introduced to a topic. Then there will be a self-rating questionnaire. This gives you a snapshot of your strength or weakness in that area. Finally, you will be provided with exercises and techniques that can permanently improve your emotional intelligence.

At this point it is up to you. If you manage yourself effectively, you can master your emotional intelligence. Do that and your life gets better.

If you manage yourself effectively, you can master your emotional intelligence.

chapter two
old maps and empty rooms

Old maps

'When you discover you are riding a dead horse the best strategy is to dismount.'

Dakota tribal saying

For a moment try a brief thought experiment. Imagine that you have gone to a town for the first time. You try and find your way around the town with an *A–Z* that is 30 years out of date. How would you do? The chances are that at times you would have few problems. However, at other times you may find it impossible to get around. You read the map and follow it, yet you cannot reach your destination. You may be frustrated and angry. This type of response is not good for your health. At other times you may just quit. You cannot find the place so you stop trying.

When you consider this scenario it seems improbable. Who would try and get around a town with an old map? Who could be so foolish? Yet we have a psychological map for 'getting around our social world'. This map includes directions on understanding ourselves, others and what to do in a variety of situations. These psychological maps are developed as we grow up. When they are accurate we can read the world well and achieve the results that we desire.

However, in many situations our psychological maps resemble the 30-year-old *A–Z*. The results can often be deeply frustrating and result in disappointments, frustrations and a sense of failure.

A room without chairs

This is a popular children's game played at parties. Several chairs are distributed throughout a room. Then a couple of children are taken to the end of the room and blindfolded. They are told that they must walk from one side of the room to another without bumping into the chairs. Once the children are blindfolded, all the chairs are removed from the room and the floor is clear. The children then tentatively move slowly across the room. They move very slowly and are understandably cautious. On occasions the children will not move at all.

Here the children have a mental map of the room. They walk across the room using this map. However, the map is inaccurate. Similarly, many people make assumptions about the world that will inhibit their performance. These are not real obstacles. They are imaginary yet appear real to the people involved. One of the challenges for us is to differentiate between imaginary and real obstacles. It is about getting a truer view of the real world.

One of the challenges for us is to differentiate between imaginary and real obstacles.

There are many ways that old maps cause problems. For example, many people do not understand their own strengths and weaknesses. So a person who overestimates their current abilities may end up experiencing an unnecessary failure. Conversely, there are many talented people who do not recognize their own talents. Their 'map of the world' tells them they have no talent and they act accordingly.

There are also people who cannot read the emotions of others. They risk appearing insensitive and miss out on valuable information. Others may not have a clear sense of purpose or of where they are going in life. In all these areas, and many others, the problems arise from having inadequate psychological maps. If you have such maps then it becomes very difficult to manage yourself. Fortunately, you can learn how to change your psychological maps of the world. In the remainder of this chapter you will get some advice on how your mind works and the learning processes linked to personal change.

When I click my fingers you'll think you are Elvis

Other names for your psychological maps of the world are beliefs or values. Whatever they are called, they exert a huge influence on the results you get in life. And even on the very quality of your life.

I have often watched shows where the stage hypnotist clicks his fingers and the member of the audience sings like Elvis or clucks like a chicken or behaves strangely. While this may be entertaining the hypnosis process also offers insights into how our minds work.

There are many scientific studies in which hypnosis is used to plant a new belief or a new map in the mind of a person. Lou Tice of the Pacific Institute described how in an elegant experiment people are hypnotized and told that a small everyday object, such as a pen, is extremely heavy and impossible to lift off a table.

Once this has been done, the person is brought out of their trance. They are asked to lift the pen off the table. They try to do so but fail. They struggle in vain. When asked why they are not lifting the pen the person says they want to but cannot do it. They are consciously trying to lift it and are perplexed at their failure to do so!

When researchers use electronic equipment to measure muscle activity a strange effect is observed. First, the person's biceps are actively trying to lift the pen. They are aware of this effort. However, in another part of the body the triceps are working to keep the pen on the table. The person is not consciously aware of this muscular activity. Within each participant there is a strong unconscious desire to behave in a way consistant with the hypnotically planted belief. This causes them to behave in ways that they do not consciously recognize.

Many of our psychological maps of the world are developed when we are young. They become part of our thinking processes. As they develop through time they go in at a deep level. They are planted so deep within us that we are not conscious of them and how they control us.

'Until we make the unconscious conscious it will rule our life and we will call it fate.'

Carl Jung

The beliefs have a direct impact on what we think, feel and perceive. In this way the beliefs directly influence the results we get in life. The diagram below illustrates the relationship between the important elements of how your mind works.

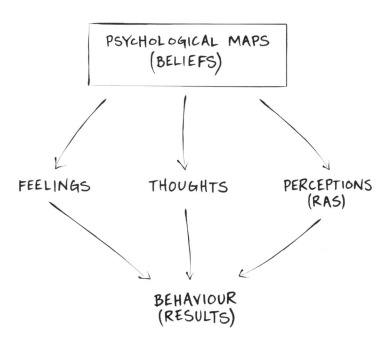

Let's take a little time to unpick the ideas behind this.

Thoughts

Take a couple of minutes to reflect upon the following questions:

◆ What thoughts do you have when something goes wrong in your life?

◆ What thoughts do you have when something pleasurable happens?

◆ What thoughts do you have when learning something new?

The thoughts that you have in response to these and other situations are sometimes called 'self-talk'. Different people will have different thoughts in similar situations. The thoughts arise from the interaction between your beliefs (maps) and the situations you find yourself in. For example, if you have a low level of confidence and you are asked to take on a challenge your self-talk will tend to be negative. You will think about the reasons why you cannot rise to the challenge. You may have thoughts anticipating failure. Likewise, you may be very creative at thinking of reasons why you should not take on the challenge.

Ironically, all this psychological activity confirms your belief that you are not up to the job. It is a vicious spiral. A negative self-fulfilling prophecy. These thinking patterns will have a direct impact upon your performance and the results you get in life.

These thinking patterns will have a direct impact upon your performance and the results you get in life.

Feelings

A simple and very useful way of understanding our feelings and emotions is by using the concept of 'the comfort zone'. This may be thought of as a psychological area or zone. Within this zone are all the thoughts and activities that allow a person to feel comfortable.

The thoughts, activities and behaviours that cause unpleasant feelings lie outside the comfort zone. The more a person moves away from familiar, comfortable activities the greater their discomfort.

There are many ways the discomfort is experienced emotionally. People may fear things outside their comfort zone. They may be anxious about certain thoughts or behaviours. They may speak of being 'stressed out'. When a person moves outside their comfort zone they may experience a wide range of physical responses, such as:

◆ panic attacks

◆ poor physical co-ordination

◆ palpitations

◆ memory loss

◆ nausea

◆ perspiration

◆ dry mouth

◆ low energy

◆ fainting.

A common experience of going outside a comfort zone comes at the time of examinations. The student may be very knowledgeable. They may have successfully completed essays and projects. Yet when they have to perform under examination conditions they move outside their comfort zone. This can result in them being nauseous and fuzzy headed and suffering memory loss. The bottom line is that they will perform poorly.

Conversely, a less gifted student whose comfort zone includes doing exams will perform at the top of their capability range and may outperform a cleverer student. We see here that EI influences results as much as, possibly more than, IQ.

In the case of the two students, the key point is why one student feels comfortable and another does not? We can trace this back to the psychological maps they possess. If old maps that deliver poor results can be changed, then life can be improved. This book will provide you with the tools to make these changes. It will enable you to 'Manage Yourself' more effectively.

Perceptions

We are able to take in and process information through our five senses. The visual, auditory, and kinesthetic (touch) are the dominant ones. However, at times both smell and taste may be very important. Each of us has a huge capacity to take in masses of information. Indeed, there could be a danger of overload. Try the following activity:

1 Notice your eyes picking up these words on the page.

2 Also notice what is in your peripheral vision.

3 Now become aware of all the sounds around you – near and far.

4 What lights and colours and shades can you see as you read?

5 How are your feet arranged? Can you feel the ground beneath them?

6 What is your body temperature?

7 Is your body temperature the same throughout your body?

8 Finally, think about 1–7 all at the same time!

Most people would respond by saying they could not process this amount of information. Yet they are receiving these inputs. They just cannot consciously deal with it all at the same time. So how do we cope? Fortunately, we have a reticular activating system (RAS).

The RAS is part of a brain that acts as a filter. It makes us aware of things that are important to us while filtering out the less important stuff. How does the RAS know what is important? It uses our maps and beliefs. These set the priorities and then the RAS works on 'autopilot'.

This process explains why people living near an airport will sleep through aeroplane take-offs and landings yet will be woken by the quieter cries of their baby. Here people believe that waking up for their child's cry is important while waking for aeroplanes is not. It is by this process that we can filter out the noise of a party yet still hear someone saying our name or talking about something we value.

The RAS allows into our conscious mind information consistent with current beliefs. If it allowed contradictory information in a person would feel uncomfortable. So the RAS is designed to minimize these bad feelings. Conversely, it readily lets in information that supports a belief. The problem arises here if the person has a belief that holds them back – a belief that is based on their opinions rather than reality. Here the belief is an old map. It is like the child assuming the chairs exist where they do not.

If a person believes that they are boring they will only perceive information that may support that point of view. Any contrary evidence will be filtered out. The RAS will prevent the person from seeing or hearing any signs of people being interested in them. The evidence of their senses means that their beliefs are never changed. There is nothing provoking change.

How the model works

In the scenarios below you can take a look at the way two people with diametrically opposite psychological maps respond to the same situation.

Case study

Bob has a strong belief that he is a capable and talented public speaker. His friend, Tom, has a different psychological map. He believes that he is an inadequate public speaker. They are both asked to make a public presentation at an important conference. How will they respond?

	Bob	Tom
Map	Talented speaker	Inadequate speaker
Thoughts	Positive anticipation Confidence Keen anticipation	Negative Doubting Worry (Memory loss on the day)
Feelings	Joy Happiness	Fear Anxiety
(On the day)	Sense of pleasure and relaxed	Palpitations Dry mouth Sweats/shaking
Perception	Seeing positive responses Perceiving ways to do a good job	Seeing negative responses Perceiving problems
Behaviour (Results)	No psychological barriers to a good presentation	Considerable psychological barriers to a good presentation

It is clear that the results in our lives are profoundly influenced by the elements of this model. If the model were inflexible you would have problems. Fortunately, people are capable of changing this model and changing their lives. So let's take a look at how people learn.

Quadrant II

One of the most exciting approaches to self-management and learning is called Quadrant II. It was developed for Quantumcoaching.co.uk (an organization specializing in developing sports coaching and athletic performance) for applications in sport.

It can be applied to all walks of life. Let's see how it applies to you. Work through the brief activities listed below – take five minutes to write in your answers:

1 Make some brief notes of your typical thoughts and feelings when you have to learn something you think you cannot do.

THOUGHTS

FEELINGS

2 How do you respond when learning is difficult and you have to do it?

3 How do you respond when learning is difficult and you don't have to do it?

Now that you have answered these questions we will run through a well known model of learning and then see how this relates to Quadrant II and your own performance improvements.

Four stage model

It is possible to look at a four stage model of learning. This is a well known way of understanding the learning process. The four stages are:

1 Unconscious incapability

2 Conscious incapability

3 Conscious capability

4 Unconscious capability.

Unconscious incapability

This occurs when a person is not aware that they are incapable of a task or skill. Often this is because the specific challenge has not arisen. Sometimes the person deludes themselves that they are capable when they are not.

Conscious incapability

Here, the person is aware that they are incapable of a task/skill. Often this results from a new challenge. When the learner has to take on the learning challenge they are prone to panic or anxiety. If they have a choice they will tend to avoid unpleasant panic/anxiety situations. At times this is called a Fight or Flight occurrence. (Fight through and learn or take Flight and get away.) If you are learning something that takes time you have to suffer for longer. In these circumstances many people will retreat or quit.

Conscious capability

Here, the learner is capable of the new skill as long as they think about performing it. They know they can do it as long as they keep it in mind. There is no panic here because the person knows they have sufficient capability.

Unconscious capability

In this fourth stage, the learner can perform the task without thinking about it. It can be done automatically. Here, thinking about how something is done may make it worse.

There is an alternative way of representing these stages (in a series of quadrants):

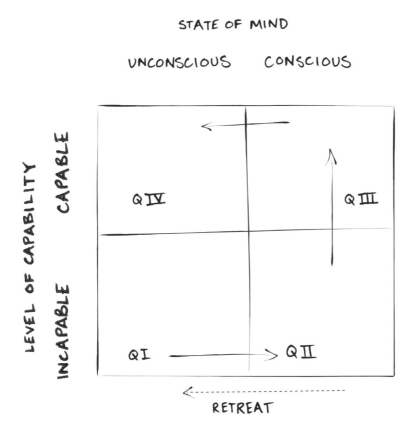

STATE OF MIND

UNCONSCIOUS   CONSCIOUS

LEVEL OF CAPABILITY — CAPABLE / INCAPABLE

Q IV   Q III

Q I ———→ Q II

RETREAT

To learn new skills or techniques means that you must enter Quadrant II. Yet this is the place where there can be most anxiety/panic/unpleasant feelings. These are stress-related emotions. For many people they respond by retreating and avoiding the learning experience; they quit. Perhaps there are areas where you could improve where you have retreated or where you would not take on a challenge.

When a person does not have unconscious mastery they may slip back to QIII. Here they have to concentrate on performing a skill so their conscious brain loses some of its ability to focus on immediate challenges. They lose track and underperform. It is possible for a person to slip further back to QII and, once there, they will think themselves incapable and all may be lost.

So QIV is desirable. Unfortunately, the anxiety at QII often prevents progress to the higher levels of QIV. This is because people believe their potential to change is limited. They have no way of dealing with the negative emotions in QII.

Managing yourself through Quadrant II

If you are going to change the quality of your life then you may need to change the way you think, feel and behave. In other words, you are going to have to learn new thoughts, feelings and behaviours. This may take you into Quadrant II. While I do not wish to reinforce the axiom of 'no pain – no gain', it is likely that going through Quadrant II will be uncomfortable. It is precisely this discomfort that causes many people to quit. Ironically, as soon as they quit the pain goes and they feel better. This reinforces their decision to retreat.

When people retreat from Quadrant II they return to their old ways of living. They are often unhappy in this state. That is why they tried changing in the first place. So staying put leads to suffering and so does changing. It seems a little like a Catch 22 situation. You suffer if you do not change and you suffer, usually more acutely, if you enter Quadrant II. It is here that two concepts can be helpful. They are clearly explained in the work of Scott Peck and are summarized in the following sections.

Life is suffering

This is one of the four Buddhist truths. At first it may appear a very pessimistic, even depressing, thing to say. However, it is a reality check. Take a look at everyone's life. At times there is difficulty. At times there is suffering. This ranges between the traumas of things like bereavement or redundancy through to being delayed on a train or temporarily losing your keys at home.

When we seek to deny that there are pains and problems we make things worse. They keep happening and we keep resisting or resenting these events. If, however, we accept that the nature of life will involve these problems, then they do not hit us quite as hard and we can do something about them. That's life.

Neurotic and existential pain

'That's life that is – think on.'

Victoria Wood

I know this heading looks like we're heading for a philosophy lesson. Fear not. Instead, it is an excellent way to think about the 'life is suffering' concept.

When you experience psychological pain or suffering you may think about the nature of it. Are you repeating the same old discomfort yet again? Is it a pattern in your life? If it is a pain that is a perennial part of your life and you have learned to accept it then it is neurotic pain. It is a form of neurosis in which you put up with your discomfort. You passively tolerate it. This ongoing psychological suffering is comparable with someone who has a chronic illness; one that continues through a long period of time.

Conversely, there is existential psychological pain. Here you have the pain that comes with making changes and developing. It is comparable with the physical pain and stiffness you may feel as you do physical training. If you focus on the pain in your muscles you may quit. If you focus upon being fitter and healthier you may persist and reap the rewards. For psychological development the pain in Quadrant II can be acute. It may hit you hard. For a short time it feels worse than the chronic/ neurotic pain. It is at this point that many people retreat.

Now you have a choice when making changes in the way you manage yourself. First, recognize that either way there may be difficult and painful consequences. Second, decide whether you want the existential pain linked with growing, developing and being happier or whether you want the chronic, neurotic pain of staying in a state of dissatisfaction. There is no magic technique here. It's about making adult choices.

There is no magic technique here. It's about making adult choices.

This is a challenge. Some of the techniques covered in chapter four will give additional ways of tolerating existential pain to be enable you to move towards Quadrants III and IV.

Control central

One of the most important psychological concepts for people interested in managing themselves is the locus of control. This measures the extent to which a person attributes the results in their life to internal or external factors.

When things go wrong in your life, are you inclined to blame other people or external events? Do you attribute it to things outside yourself? In these circumstances the person is said to have an external locus of control. With an external locus of control people take only a limited amount of responsibility for their lives. They tend to be passive and rarely take the initiative. There is a tendency to sit and wait for the world to change so that their lives may change.

Those people with a strong internal locus of control have a tendency to take responsibility for the results they get in their lives. They are proactive. They believe that if their life is to improve they must take action themselves.

The research shows that people with a higher internal locus of control tend to be happier, have a higher level of achievement and a higher quality of life.

How are you doing? How would you rate your locus of control?

How are you doing? How would you rate your locus of control?

Zone of concern

'God grant me the serenity to accept the things I cannot change, the courage to change the things I can, and the wisdom to know the difference.'

Reinhold Niebuhr

A convenient way to think about your locus of control and your way of looking at the world is to use a concept called 'the zone of concern'. Here you can define all the areas of your life within a large zone: the zone of concern. Within this zone you may have three further sub-zones. One is a zone of control. This covers the concerns that you control. The second zone is one of influence. In this zone will be concerns that you do not control but can influence. Those areas in your zone of concern that you cannot control or influence are concerns outside of your control, which are known as the 'non-control' zone. Here is an example zone of concern.

Control	Influence	Non-control
eating	friends	boss/partner
bit of studying	own emotions	career/most of finances
5% of time	5% of time	90% of time

The example above would be more likely to represent a person with a low internal locus of control. Most of the control in the person's life is perceived as external. For a person with a higher internal locus of control the control and influence areas would be far larger and the non-control area would be smaller.

In the zone of concern below, list the 10 most important aspects of your life. Pencil them into the box. If half are under your control then 50 per cent of this box will be a zone of control. If only one item is in your control, then only 10 per cent of the box will be zone of control.

Control	Influence	Non-control

For those areas you define outside your control, try and identify ways you can control them or take control of small elements of them. You can also identify how other people may control those areas you define as out of control; could you emulate those people?

It is evident that people who have a high quality of life invariably have large zones of control and influence.

When we look at all the research on emotional intelligence it is undeniable that each element is controllable. This means that you have the power to boost your EI and improve the quality of your life. I may try and influence you with this book but ultimately the choice is yours. It depends on how you choose to 'Manage Yourself'.

Now that you have some ideas on how you learn and change, the next chapter takes a look at the most important elements of emotional intelligence and reveals how you can master them.

03

chapter three
self-awareness – it's a wonderful life

It's a wonderful life

In Frank Capra's classic film *It's a Wonderful Life* George Bailey, played by James Stewart, is given a unique opportunity. He is on the verge of committing suicide when a guardian angel intercedes. Stewart's character believes his life has been a failure. Such is the strength of this belief that it dominates his thoughts and feelings. They become increasingly negative. His beliefs also shape his perceptions. He sees failure everywhere and feels there is no reason to go on with life.

The guardian angel makes it possible for Stewart to see how the world would be if he had never existed. It becomes more and more obvious that Stewart has enriched the lives of many people. He gradually appreciates the impact that he has had upon the world. With this new awareness Stewart's thoughts, feelings and perceptions change. He is happier. He wants to live again.

The film provides an excellent example of a man who lacks self-awareness. He is a good and decent man. A talented man. However, he lacked self-awareness. Later he got some, thanks to an angel.

Many people operate in the world with little or no understanding of themselves. This lack of understanding may apply to several different aspects of life. These include:

- awareness of your beliefs
- awareness of your capabilities
- awareness of your skills and knowledge
- awareness of your thoughts and emotions.

One of the difficulties is that we are not aware of the things we are not aware of! We often have blind spots in those areas where we can make the most significant improvement.

Blind spots and Johari Windows

In chapter two we covered the notion of maps and beliefs. When we understand these beliefs we can then appreciate how they influence the results we get in life. We can be aware of how they impact upon our day-to-day lives. However, there are many times that we have blind spots. We are unaware of beliefs, thoughts and feelings that reduce the quality of our lives. We are highly adept at seeing other people's blind spots but are very poor at recognizing our own blind spots.

An easy way to gain an insight into blind spots is to try the exercise below. Simply read through it once and count the 'F's. It may be worth asking a few friends to go through the same process.

Finished files are the result of years of scientific
study combined with the experience of many years.

How many did you count? There are six in total yet many people only count three or four. If you got several people to do it, you will probably have found that most of them count less than six. They are blind to some of the 'F's. Why do you think so many people have these blind spots? The explanation is very straightforward: many people are taught to read phonetically. This means that the word 'of' is pronounced 'ov'. So when we are looking for 'F's we may not see any in the word we read as 'ov'.

This is an excellent illustration of how the way we learn can influence our actual perceptions. We are never taught to be blind. It is a consequence of our learning. So the challenge is to become aware of these blind spots.

At this point we can use the Johari Window technique. This may seem to be an exotic name – it was actually invented by two guys called Joe and Harry (thus Joe-Harry). The technique can be illustrated diagrammatically:

```
                              OTHERS
                    SEE              CAN'T SEE

              ┌──────────────────┬──────────────────┐
              │                  │                  │
        SEE   │     PUBLIC       │     PRIVATE      │
              │                  │                  │
 SELF         ├──────────────────┼──────────────────┤
              │                  │                  │
   CAN'T SEE  │   BLIND SPOT     │      DEEP        │
              │                  │   UNCONSCIOUS    │
              └──────────────────┴──────────────────┘
```

In the windows of the matrix there are two categories of people; you (self) and everyone else (others).There are two further sub-categories; those things that people are aware of (see) and are not aware of (can't see).

First of all there are things that the person and the others all see. These are the *public* aspects of the person. Then there are those aspects of a person that they themselves can see, but others cannot. Here we have the person's *private* world. Sometimes information can move from private to public because the person confides in people they trust. There are also times when the private becomes public due to a slip of the tongue!

The third category has an important role in personal development. This addresses those areas where the public are aware of things about the person that they themselves cannot see. The person has a *blind spot*. A simple example of this would be a person with bad breath who does not recognize it while other people do. Most people will have behavioural blind spots. Naturally, it is impossible to do anything about your weak areas if you are blind to them. There needs to be awareness and this may be possible through feedback.

Finally, there is that area that the individual and others are both unable to see. Here something may 'pop out' in dreams or sudden thoughts. This is the area that might be probed by psychiatrists and psychotherapists. It is the area of the *deep unconscious*.

By asking yourself questions, and reflecting on your life, you are able to get a grasp of the public and private areas. If you are willing to collect feedback from other people, you may start to discover your blind spots. The blind spots provide insights into the old maps and beliefs that may be holding you back. Another way of accessing the things that you can't see is to use psychometric tests. These may cost a little money but they are useful tools through which to gain self-awareness.

In most cases, the probing and questioning of the 'can't see' areas is stressful and painful. But take heart, it is existential pain. If you persevere you will reap the benefits. So learn to tough it out.

Levels of emotional awareness

One of the leading researchers in emotional intelligence is Dr John Mayer. He has identified three broad levels of emotional self-awareness – self-aware, engulfed and accepting. As you read through their descriptions, decide on which are best applied to you.

Self-aware

Some people have a sophisticated awareness and understanding of their emotional lives. They are very clear on feelings, moods and emotions. This provides a solid foundation for managing emotions.

Engulfed

Some people are swamped and pulled around on a sea of emotions. These people are helpless and their behaviour is driven by their moods. There is a strong sense of being overwhelmed.

Accepting

Some people are able to identify their emotions. They are resigned to those emotions. When the emotion is positive the person is happy.

However, when the emotions are negative they are not so good. There is a sense that emotions simply happen and the person responds accordingly.

These varying levels of self-awareness are not abstract concepts. They describe the ways people live. The scenarios below show the practical ways varying levels of self-awareness influence our day-to-day lives.

Case study

Matt is having increasing problems in his life. He works in a small software company in a position of responsibility. He lives with his partner and their four-year-old daughter. Matt is in a cycle of powerful emotions and behaviours. He works long hours to 'get on top of his job'. He gets tired and has little energy left for home life. This leads to tensions and emotional pulls from his family. He has no time for friends and his wider family. An outside observer will see Matt on an emotional rollercoaster. He is at times 'depressed' and lethargic, while at other times he is 'hyperactive'. He may be very quick to anger or seems unmoved by important events. He seems unclear how events affect him and how he may be performing.

Chris Daniels was a successful international athlete. He had enjoyed a long and illustrious career. In his final year of playing he became the assistant coach at his club. The results were disastrous. He regularly lost his temper with players. Daniels was convinced that his players were lazy or stupid or just plain awkward. At first the focus was on these surface explanations and the heated emotions. However, one of the reasons for his failure was that he did not know how to organize and arrange coaching sessions. Nor did he appreciate that what he could do 'naturally' may be impossible for lesser players. Once those deficits were addressed things improved.

Sandra has a clear understanding of her emotions and what triggers them. When she works with certain people she is happy and willing to take on challenges. Some people, including her line manager, cause her to feel bad and depressed.

There are also certain tasks at home and at work that adversely influence her mood. Sandra is crystal clear on her emotional likes and dislikes. She just hopes to be with the right people, jobs or activities.

Sunna has a high level of self-awareness. She is very clear on her technical skills in the workplace. She does not achieve this by accident. It is done by being willing to ask for, and listen to, feedback. This feedback is sought from people able to provide good, quality information. This level of activity requires a high level of commitment to truth and a willingness to hear less than flattering feedback. Sunna is also self-aware of her emotional experiences and responses. This extends beyond knowing how her emotions interact with external events. Sunna is also aware that it is possible to make changes when the emotion she experiences has an adverse impact on the quality of her life.

In the latter cases the level of awareness makes it possible to make changes that lead to a happier and more successful life.

Where we lack awareness – conscious recognition – we allow the unconscious patterns to control our destiny.

In our daily lives a lack of self-awareness means we are blind to key influences on the quality of our lives. Where we lack awareness – conscious recognition – we allow the unconscious patterns to control our destiny. So far we have concentrated on the aspects of self-awareness that focus upon understanding ourselves as we are now. The exercises later in this chapter will help you to deepen this understanding. There is a second, closely linked, aspect of self-awareness. That is the awareness you have of the life you wish to live. This aspect concerns your awareness of your purpose in life and how you will create that future. This will be explored in detail in the next chapter.

How do you feel?

A useful activity when developing self-awareness is to start to define your own emotions. You can define them in a way that is meaningful to you. Once you have done this, you can precisely define the physical experience you have when in a particular emotional state. For example, when you are in a state of fear think about what you feel. Do you have a sensation in the body? Where is it? What shape is it? What is its intensity? How long does it go on for? What is your breathing like?

By asking these and other questions you are able to become increasingly aware of your emotional states. As you work through this process you can also combine it with keeping a record of your thought patterns. When you experience a particular emotion, what do you say to yourself? One thing or many things? Do certain thoughts go around in your head repeating themselves?

As you undertake this rigorous process you will be able to explore the way your thoughts and emotions are linked. You will also be able to identify things that trigger your responses.

As time goes by

A further way of enhancing your self-awareness is to become mindful of the ways you use your time. Often people drift through days – even lives! They are conscious of doing certain things while many other activities are done on autopilot. By systematically keeping a time log you are able to see where your time goes. If this is done over several weeks you can see where your time is going. You can then decide whether it is the way you want to live. It is possible to identify the things on which you procrastinate and where your time is wasted. If you are not living the life you want to live, it is up to you to make changes.

If you are not living the life you want to live, it is up to you to make changes.

The DREC curve

When you are making changes in your life you are likely to experience the DREC curve. This is a useful model for explaining the psychological stages we experience when we go through change. These may be changes that are internally generated such as when we set future goals – we are choosing to change and then move in that direction. So a specific outcome has been pre-selected in this case.

The second type of catalysts for change are externally generated. In this type, something in our environment changes and it becomes impossible for the person to be unmoved. Typical large-scale events that kick start change include bereavement, divorce and redundancy. There are generally four feelings / responses to such events, which are detailed below.

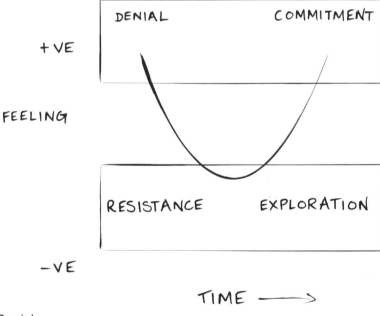

Denial

The first response to imposed changes, or the need for change, is often denial. Here it is difficult to accept that change is required. At times the person goes on behaving in the old way. So the bereaved wife continues to iron her husband's clothes or the redundant worker still gets up and gets ready for work. There is a tendency to focus on the past. This is how it always was. This is where it feels comfortable. Here people can also be numbed and apathetic.

Resistance

As denial fades there is a realization that the old ways of being and behaving may no longer be tenable. At this stage the numbness gives way to more observable emotional responses. The person may experience emotions such as rage, anger, anxiety, panic, sadness and depression. When someone loses their job they may be very resentful and agitated. Conversely, they could be despondent and resigned to a 'sense of failure'. Other symptoms include disturbed sleep and a sense of impotence. Here people know the old ways have gone, yet resist letting go of them.

Exploration

In the third stage there is an elevation in the levels of energy. People switch their attention from the past and present towards the future. At times the energy is channelled into many directions and 'projects'. Here the person is trying to capture some control over their lives and their destiny. There may be a tendency towards dense, overelaborate solutions. There may be difficulty in concentrating on a single approach. The lack of progress may be frustrating. However, the mood of the person is elevated and they become more proactive. A typical example will be a redundant person who starts applying for a variety of jobs, explores self-employment and checks out retraining all at the same time.

Commitment

The final stage of the transition process is commitment. The person has now found new patterns of behaviour and has energy to channel into them. At this stage there are subtle refinements. There is a clear sense of direction. There is also a sense of making real progress.

DREC and QII

'Nothing in the world can take the place of persistence. Talent will not; nothing is more common than an unsuccessful man with talent. Genius will not; unrewarded genius is almost a proverb. Education alone will not; the world is full of educated derelicts. Persistence and determination alone are omnipotent.'

Calvin Coolidge

It is worth looking at the DREC model and the Quadrant model as it is useful to match the components of one model with those of the other. (D=Q1, R=Q2, E=Q3, C=Q4). In the DREC model the biggest challenge is to work through the resistance phase. This is comparable with experiences that people have in Quadrant II. In both cases the person needs to keep going. As they do so, they will move into the next stage and immediately begin to feel better.

You can apply your understanding of these models as you manage yourself and master your emotional intelligence. They apply to a person going through a cognitive or emotional change. If you identify lower levels of emotional intelligence you may experience resistance and a desire to retreat. However, if you apply the exercise activities in this book you will be able to move through exploration and commitment.

One of the great things about emotional intelligence is that progress in one area often leads to progress in another. Certainly the elements of emotional intelligence will help you work through the DREC model. For example, self-awareness may indicate whether a person is in denial. The clear definition of a purpose and goals leads to a more rapid move to commitment. By being creative you will have more options during exploration. The emotional management options of persistence and resilience help you to tolerate the pain of transition and to keep going.

Activities

Now it is time for you to get stuck into some activities. It is time to take action. And I don't mean the action of reading through the activities and then going on to the next chapter. There are those people who do such activities and actually write them down in the book, while a few others make notes elsewhere. Finally, there are those who never really get around to doing the activities. Sadly, this final group of people never fulfil their potential, no matter how many developmental books they read. Even by making quick notes you increase your chances of success. So do it. Start by completing the self-rating scale below.

1 Where are you now? Self-rating

Score yourself on the scale from 1–10

10 = Total agreement
1 = Total disagreement

SELF-AWARENESS	SCORE
◆ I am aware of my feelings most of the time.	_____
◆ I can clearly define my strengths and weaknesses.	_____
◆ I can identify and name my different emotions.	_____
◆ I know my developmental needs for the short and long term.	_____
◆ I know which situations cause me to feel anger, calm and joy.	_____
◆ I notice my physical state to understand my feelings.	_____
◆ I am never completely swamped by my emotions.	_____
◆ I am responsible for how I feel.	_____
TOTAL	

A key to the self-rating scale

The self-rating scales aim to offer a quick insight into your capability in each emotional intelligence area. First calculate your score and then take a look at the key. This key can be used for all the self-rating scales in this book.

65+   You need only focus upon honing your skills.

40–64   Actions taken here would improve the quality of your life.

Under 40   Your low score here indicates an element of EI that may be
            significantly undermining the quality of your life. You would benefit
            from taking immediate and decisive action.

2 What do you believe?

If you ask most people if they have ever sat quietly for half an hour and thought about their beliefs and emotions few would have done so. Yet this is an easy way to improve your emotional intelligence. Work through the questions below and write your answers in the spaces provided. Always be honest with yourself.

(i)   I believe I am good at . . .

(ii) I believe I am poor at . . .

(iii) I believe that to be successful you must . . .

(iv) I believe to be happy you must . . .

(v) I believe that my life would be better if . . .

(vi) Briefly make notes about your beliefs on love, friendship, work, your ability to understand other people, your ability to judge character and how you respond to adversity.

(vii) Where possible, review points (i) to (vi) with other people. What do they think are your beliefs? This may be done systematically by asking them about each point. Do their answers match yours: Do you have any blind spots?

(viii) Can you see the ways your beliefs shape your life? Which beliefs, if any, would you change (and why)?

As you review your beliefs, think back to the model of you in chapter two (see page 17). What are the likely thoughts, feelings and perceptions that are derived from your beliefs? How will all these elements combine to shape your life? Imagine what it would be like if you changed one of these beliefs for a day, a week, a year. How would your life change?

3 What do you feel?

Now that you have spent time focusing on your beliefs, let's get stuck in to your emotions and feelings. This will help you to define your feelings and think about where they come from.

(a) (i) Make a list of five of the most common emotions you experience.

(ii) For each emotion, can you outline the precise physical experience you notice when it occurs? (To help you to do this, ask yourself what do you feel? When did you feel it? How big was the feeling? How long did you feel it for?)

Emotion	Description
1	
2	
3	
4	
5	

(b) (i) List the five emotions a second time.

(ii) First time, can you identify people/situations/events that trigger each emotion?

Emotion	Description
1	
2	
3	
4	
5	

(c) For each emotion, try to explain why the trigger leads to the emotion. Ask yourself why several times as you search for the reasons.

Let's take a look at what this exercise can look like in practice.

Sample response

EMOTION	DESCRIPTION
Anxiety	Heart pounding, nausea, left hand shakes, mouth dry.

EMOTION	TRIGGER
Anxiety	Whenever I'm assessed by another person.

EXPLANATION

I don't like being assessed.

Why?

I might fail.

Why does that cause anxiety?

I don't like failing.

Why?

Because I believe people will think I am stupid.

Why does that concern you?

Because I'm insecure.

A second way of seeking an explanation is to go back to the model of you. When you define the feelings then go on to describe the thoughts and perceptions. Once you have all three, ask yourself: which belief/beliefs lead to these outcomes?

At this stage we haven't yet looked at how you can manage your emotions. However, the increased awareness you have now will still reduce the likelihood of you being engulfed by your emotions. The process of analysis puts you more in control.

4 What do you think?

We have tackled beliefs and feelings. Now let's look at a technique for exploring your thinking.

(a) For a day, try and notice any times when you are experiencing very positive or very negative self-talk.

(b) Identify the triggers to these bouts of self-talk.

(c) Are there any ways you could increase the positives and reduce the negatives?

Here again the analysis puts you in control. You will begin to recognize patterns of behaviour. You may wish to repeat positive patterns. However, if you have detected negative patterns you are now in a position to start changing them. Remember you control them not vice versa!

5 Keep a time log

So far you have explored aspects of yourself (beliefs/feelings/thoughts). In this exercise you take a look at the big picture. Where does your time go? Is it spent wisely on the really important things in life? At many times in our lives it is a great skill to focus upon the 'now' rather than be distracted by the past and future. However, by focusing in this way we can miss the big picture. This exercise and the personal diaries exercise, which comes next, both provide you with a wider perspective. They enable you to become aware of patterns that only manifest themselves through time.

(a) For at least a week, keep a time log. Simply record the time of day, the activity you were involved in and its duration.

Sample log

Time	Activity	Duration
17.15	Travelling home	45 mins
18.00	Made dinner	30 mins
18.30	Ate dinner	30 mins
19.00	'Veged' out	3 hrs

(b) After a week, review your time log. Ask yourself:

◆ Is this the way I want to live?

◆ Could I make improvements?

The aim here is to provide you with some personal insights. It is not a time management exercise.

6 Personal diaries

An excellent way to increase your self-awareness is to keep a diary. In it make a daily note of the important things that happen. Be honest and open with yourself. Be willing to reflect upon your beliefs, thoughts and feelings. Also note how these relate to other people around you.

You need only spend 5–10 minutes a day on this activity. Perhaps you may allocate an hour every 2 or 3 months to read it in its entirety. While doing this you may detect patterns emerging. Many you will wish to keep. Others will be seen as barriers to greater happiness and success. These you will need to change.

7 Positive listing

A great way to improve your self-awareness is to use a technique called positive listing. Not only does it influence your self-awareness, it is also able to improve other aspects of your life.

The technique is as follows:

(a) Select a positive quality in your life that you wish to develop.

(b) Name the quality.

(c) Make a list of all the times that you have directly experienced that quality.

(d) Take each example in your list and add further details. Where were you? Who was there? What did you see, hear and feel?

So, if you want to increase your self-awareness of confidence, do a list of all the times you felt confidence. This may be in small situations as well as large. By doing this you give clearer instructions to your brain as to what exactly being confident really means. Also, by repeatedly thinking this way you make yourself more likely to think and feel that way in the future.

One further advantage of positive listing is that it reinforces the notion that you choose your thoughts and feelings. In most of our lives we are not being hit by huge, earth shattering external events. Instead we live our usual day-to-day existence. We are able to choose our thoughts. Yet much of the time thoughts and feelings just seem to 'pop into our heads'. By using positive listing we get into the habit of 'chasing our thoughts'.

Moving on

These exercises will have helped you to take control of your life as it now is. In the next chapter we will look at ways you can define and create the life you desire.

04

chapter four
goal setting – step forward
Julie Andrews

'Climb every mountain
Ford every stream
Follow every rainbow
Until you find your dream.'

Lyric from *The Sound of Music*

One of the best researched areas of emotional intelligence is goal setting. If you are serious about managing yourself and improving the quality of your life, then this chapter will be vitally important. There is a stack of evidence that shows that goal setting improves your performance. The differences between the goal setter and the non-goal setter are staggering. However, it is possible to select and set goals in such a way as to get even better results. You will be shown these cutting edge approaches later in the chapter.

The Yale experience

One of the most fascinating anecdotal examples of goal setting concerns Yale University and it is described in many personal development books. Robin Sieger provides one of the clearest descriptions of what happened. He tells us that in the 1950s a questionnaire was sent to 1,500 Yale students. It asked them a wide range of questions. The last two questions were: 'Do you have an ambition for your life?' and 'Have you written it down?' Then, 25 years later a postgraduate student decided to revisit this survey. He found that 75 per cent of students had an ambition for life. However, only 3.3 per cent had written it down. He found that this small group of 51 students had been extremely successful in their lives. Far more successful than the other 97 per cent. The key explanation of this difference was that the 3.3 per cent had written goals.

In 1996 a detailed scientific study was undertaken by Edwin Locke, a Professor at the University of Maryland and co-author of *A Theory of Goal Setting and Performance*. He did a review of 30 years of academic research on goal setting and work performance. There were over 40,000 participants in these studies. The research was done in eight countries in a variety of conditions. Locke found some consistent patterns in the research.

Locke 1996: key findings

- The more specific the goal the more precise the performance.
- Specific and challenging goals lead to high performance.
- Personal commitment to goals is necessary when they are specific and challenging.
- Feedback showing progress towards goals aids the process.
- Commitment to goals is accentuated when:
    1 The person thinks the goal matters
    2 The person thinks the goal is achievable.

A third source that highlights the importance of goals arises out of the work of Richard Bandler and John Grinder. These two researchers became interested in discovering why some therapists achieve extraordinary results with patients, yet other therapists, using the same approach, were less effective. The research led Bandler and Grinder to create one of the most significant developments in psychology in the last 30 years – Neuro Linguistic Programming (NLP).

One of their key discoveries in NLP was that great therapists were all very good at working with patients to define well formed outcomes. This is a very precise definition and vision of what the patient will be like when they are cured. So the well formed outcome is a type of goal setting. It defines a desired future state. It is abundantly clear that the greater the precision of the goals, and the more concrete they are made, the greater their likelihood of being realized.

Just as the precision assists individuals to achieve more in their life, it also can have the same impact on companies. This is why so much energy and resources are aften dedicated to creating mission statements and vision. These are outward and visible signs of what an organization wishes to achieve. The organization takes time to try and get everyone to commit themselves to the vision. This is not psychobabble. It is smart business practice. In his book *Beyond Entrepreneurship: Turning your business into an enduringly great company*, James Collins compared organizations that had vision with those without any. Collins found that those organizations with universally grand goals outperformed their competitors by a factor of 10. In sport there is a lot of evidence that goal setting has an impact. So goal setting works.

This is not psychobabble. It is smart business practice.

Case study

In sport we are familiar with the ideas of setting goals and targets. Both coaches and athletes use these techniques to enhance performance. So sport can provide us with classic examples of goal setting.

A great example of setting stretching goals can be seen in the career of five times Olympic gold medallist Steve Redgrave. To win golds at five separate Olympic games is an awesome achievement. It is said that Redgrave was asked what went through his mind when he won his third gold medal in 1992 at Barcelona. His answer was, 'Winning the Atlanta gold in 1996'. This illustrates the single mindedness and focus of a champion.

This process ought to be done within a wider context. First, if the goal becomes an obsession it may destroy other aspects of a person's life as everything is sacrificed at the altar of a goal. At times, people sacrifice their ethics in order to achieve goals. In sport, Ben Johnson won the 100 metre gold medal at the Seoul Olympics in 1988. Sadly, he cheated. Johnson took performance enhancing drugs. Such was his desire to win that he was willing to cheat. When goal setting lacks a moral base these things can happen.

Goals and RAS

You were introduced to the reticular activating system (RAS) in chapter two. We noted how our beliefs have a direct impact upon what we filter into consciousness and what we filter out. Fortunately, there is another way to manage our perception. Start by doing the brief exercise below.

For this exercise you must not look at your watch. Draw your watch in this box. Be as precise as possible. Try and accurately draw all the details. Does it have numbers, numerals or dots? Does it have a date and maker name on the watch face? Is it the correct size?

Now compare your drawing with your watch. Rate your accuracy.

You may find some glaring inaccuracies. Certainly if you get half a dozen people to do this exercise you will see them. When you consider that you may look at your watch hundreds of times every year, it is surprising that you could get it wrong. However, we all miss things because of our RAS. When we look at our watch the goal is to see the time. This gives our brain the clear instruction to notice the time but not anything else – such as details of the timepiece. So our goals will give instructions to our RAS. If you were offered a prize of £50,000 for an accurate drawing you may have a different goal and then see more details. This shows how our goals influence our perceptions.

By setting clear goals you provide instructions to your senses to filter in important information. In life, when you have 'the goal' to buy a product you quickly notice relevant sales offers or adverts. The right information comes to your attention. When goals are vague then inputs are vague and your outcomes are . . . vague.

When goals are vague then inputs are vague and your outcomes are . . . vague.

Ethics and goals

'If your train's on the wrong track, every station you come to is the wrong station.'

Bernard Malamud

When setting goals, be sure to do it in an ethical context. Some people become so focused upon achieving a goal that they forget about doing what is right and staying within ethical boundaries. The case of Ben Johnson is one of many examples of rule breaking in the pursuit of a goal. In Britain during the 1990s the mis-selling of pensions occurred. Often sales staff were trying to hit performance goals (to keep their job or receive large bonuses). This led to thousands of people being sold policies that were not what they needed. In this case, and many others, the goal is achieved yet the long term results may be undesirable. So when you set goals keep in mind your sense of right and wrong.

One way to keep on track with goals is to make sure that they are consistent with your deepest sense of purpose.

The power of purpose

'Strong lives are motivated by dynamic purposes.'

K. Hildebrand

When setting goals and objectives, there is one further consideration. That is your purpose or your vocation. All too often people set goals based upon the desires of others. They do not set goals on what is most important to them.

Case study

Peter Demsey feels he is drifting through life. He lives from day to day. He follows reasonably regular routines. Peter's weekdays are very similar to each other. On the weekends he pursues a few leisure interests. Career-wise, Peter would be described as having plateaued.

Peter did have goals – such as to get to work on time, to have a decent pension and to have a two week holiday in Florida each year.

Dave Parks is unhappy with his life. To the outside observer he has it all. He is happily married with children, he is highly paid and holds a senior management position in a leading international company. He would describe himself as cash rich and time poor. From his early management days, Dave has systematically set goals. He sets precise goals and uses a written goal planner. When Dave reviews his goal planners from earlier years he sees that he has enjoyed systematic, consistent improvement.

Despite this success, Dave has a strong sense of dissatisfaction. Ironically, the more he continues to achieve most of his goals the difficulty deepens a little. Each year he hopes to alleviate his discontent.

Valerie Logan has a clear sense of purpose. She has a very real sense of vocation. Her abiding desire is to help underprivileged children. She works mornings in the voluntary sector in a nursery in a low income area. Valerie also raises money for children's charities with her church. It is clear to any observer that Valerie is a caring person who truly wants to help children. She recognizes that her efforts make a difference. However, Valerie has a sense of not making the impact she feels she can. She is not sure whether she is 'spreading herself too thin'. She has a sense that she has more to give.

The goals that people set may be those desired by their parents. They may be society's definitions of success and achievement. They may come from peer pressure. If they are not congruent with a person's true purpose then the achievement of these goals may make him or her more unhappy and unfulfilled. This is because in such cases the achievement of the goals is taking the person further away from what they truly want. Another consequence of unaligned goals is that the person has to force themselves to achieve the goal. It requires much more effort than something that is genuinely desired.

When there is a sense of purpose but no precise definition of outcomes and goals a person may get frustrated. They fail to make the progress they desire (such as the case with Valerie Logan). They do not have a mechanism for defining what they want and the way they will move towards getting it. So purpose without goal setting can also bring with it a fair share of frustration.

When purpose and goal setting are combined, the results can be spectacular. The working towards outcomes is energizing and exhilarating. You know what you want, you know that you definitely want it and you have a structured approach to achieving your outcome.

You know what you want, you know that you definitely want it and you have a structured approach to achieving your outcome.

An inspiring example of this combination is illustrated in the case of the Odone family, a story that was dramatized in the film *Lorenzo's Oil*. In 1984 five-year-old Lorenzo Odone was diagnosed with adreno-leuko-dystrophy (ALD). This is a degenerative disease of the nervous system. Most children with ALD do not live beyond their mid-teens. The disease is rare so it was not as thoroughly researched as other illnesses.

Lorenzo's parents were a linguist and an economist. They had no medical expertise. However, they had a son with ALD. They had the purpose of helping their son and others like him. They achieved many goals consistent with that purpose. They even made medical breakthroughs that have improved the quality of life of thousands of children worldwide. Lorenzo is 24 years old and still alive.

Who would have imagined that in the modern age non-scientists could make medical breakthroughs? Certainly not the parents of Lorenzo. Yet when they had a passionate purpose and a clearly defined set of outcomes they were successful. This is the power of purpose. In this chapter you will be helped to find your purpose and tap into your powers.

The energy and determination generated by a clear purpose have a genuine impact on our ability to learn. If you think back to Quadrant II you will remember that it can be a painful time. However when you really want to achieve a goal – like Lorenzo's parents – then you can tolerate the pain and push through to Quadrants III and IV.

Julie Andrews v. Doris Day

Before going on to the practical exercises, we need to briefly consider two conflicting self-management philosophies. They can be characterized as the Julie Andrews / Doris Day positions.

I am not being entirely accurate here. The Julie Andrews position should perhaps be called the 'Mother Superior in *The Sound of Music* position'. For brevity we'll stick with Julie! In the film when Maria

(Julie Andrews) tells her Mother Superior that she is in a quandary over her vocation, she gets some advice from the Mother Superior in the shape of a song: 'Climb every Mountain'. At the heart of the song is that it is important to find your dream (purpose). A dream that will last through time. Furthermore, there is a recognition that to find this dream may take some effort (climbing mountains and fording streams, etc). The message is clear. You should make the effort to find your vocation. Occasionally, it is thrust upon you, like it was with the Odones. However, you can become proactive when seeking your purpose.

Alternatively, you can take the Doris Day approach. Here I am picking out her song 'Que Sera Sera'. This was sung by Doris Day in an Alfred Hitchcock film! The gist of the song is 'What will be will be. The future's not ours to see.' This is a passive acceptance of things. While this may have some appeal, it does have a rather external locus of control. It gives up responsibility for creating your own life. Funnily enough no one in the film pointed this out to Doris.

Where are you on the Julie Andrews – Doris Day continuum? If you are at the Doris Day end you can go on to the next chapter. In fact, you may as well forget about all the exercises in this book. All of them presuppose that you can choose to change – rather than sticking to 'what will be will be'. If you want to manage yourself and create your future, then work through the following activities.

Activities

The evidence showing that goal setting can improve the quality of your life is undeniable. It is now time to take action. First, use the rating scale below. It will give you a snapshot of where you are and how far you may progress. Then work through the following exercises. It may take a few hours to work through. It will be a worthwhile investment of your time. Be sure to be clear on the links between purpose, goals and affirmations. By integrating them you increase their effectiveness. Be sure to build the whole process on solid ethical foundations. Select a purpose that inspires and energizes you.

1 Where are you now? Self-rating

Score yourself on the scale from 1 to 10 for each statement.

10 = Total agreement

1 = Total disagreement

PURPOSE AND GOALS	SCORE

◆ I have a clear sense of vocation.   _____

◆ I can clearly define my short, medium and long term
   goals.   _____

◆ I regularly review my goals.   _____

◆ I have taken time to define my personal vision of the
   future.   _____

◆ I am willing to sacrifice short term gains for long term
   benefits.   _____

◆ I have a passionate commitment to my goals.   _____

◆ My goals are written down.   _____

◆ My goals are specific and have timescales.   _____

TOTAL

2 Finding your purpose

The aim of this exercise is to help you to find your purpose. This has got to be the starting point of any goal setting process. By some careful reflection and thought you may quickly be able to define your purpose. Make notes in the spaces below as you work through the questions.

(a) (i) Select a positive influential person in your life.

◆ Name the person

◆ Which qualities do you most admire in that person?

◆ What do you learn from that person?

(ii) Think back over your life.

- ◆ Make notes on enjoyable times.
- ◆ What activities/hobbies lead to time 'flying by'?

(iii) Briefly describe a perfect day.

(iv) Complete the following sentence five times:
I love doing . . .

(b) Review your answers in Section (a). Think about your vocation in life. What is your strong sense of purpose? As you write down your purpose, try and ensure that:

- ◆ it has guiding principles (such as honesty, responsibility, etc)
- ◆ it represents the best you can be
- ◆ it gives you focus and you feel motivated by it.

3 Goal setting I

Your goals are the specific targets and milestones you wish to achieve. They are the ways that you will make your purpose something observable and real. The goals provide a framework for energizing yourself and switching on your RAS. They also allow you to monitor progress.

The following steps help you to set goals and objectives.

(a) Keep your purpose firmly in mind. Define precisely what your ideal world or lifestyle will be like five years from today.

(b) Check that your description is balanced. Ensure that it covers all important aspects of your life. Be sure to address your goals for your family life, career, personal health and development and other important aspects of your life.

(c) Check that your description is precise. (If you want a good car, make sure that you name the marque, describe its colour, mileage and what you will see, hear and feel when you have the car.)

(d) Check that your description is challenging and stretching. You do not want your goals to be so 'impossible' that you immediately think that they cannot be done. Select things that will lead to some internal tension. Remind yourself that this tension, this pain, is part of growing and developing.

(e) Check that your description is desirable. That you really want it.

(f) Once you have completed a–e for your five-year goals, repeat the process for three-year and one-year goals.

(g) Ensure that there is clear progression from one year through to five years.

(h) You may then repeat the process for the next week/month.

If you have defined your purpose and worked through this goal setting process thoroughly, you will have taken giant steps towards managing yourself. You will certainly improve the quality of your life.

4 Goal setting II

In this exercise, and the following one, the aim is to give you some prompts to continue the process started in Exercise 3. You are encouraged to think across several areas of your life and through an extended period of time. Be sure to put key points in the boxes provided. Try working through the table (derived from 'The Human Situation' by Harvey Jackins).

	This week	This month	This year	Five years	Always
For me					
For my family					
For my friends					
For my community					
For my country					
For humankind					
For all living things					

5 Goal setting III

It is useful to work through a similar process for work-based goals.
Fill in the table below with this in mind.

	This week	This month	This year	Five years	Always
For me					
For my customers					
For my friends					
For my boss					
For my team					
For my department					
For my organization					

6 Affirmations

Once you have all your goals you are ready to go on to affirmations.
This technique allows you to imprint your goals and desires on your
brain. This is done by creating short, powerful statements and
reviewing them regularly.
An affirmation is a positive sentence that describes the way you
want to be. It should provide a bridge from your purpose to a

specific aspect of performance. Each affirmation sentence should be written on a card and use the following guidelines. The affirmation should be:

♦ *Personal*
  The affirmation should describe what you want for yourself rather than anyone else.
♦ *Positive*
  The affirmation should describe what you want (positive) rather than what you don't want (negative).
♦ *Present tense*
  The affirmation should be written as if you already have the quality: 'I am confident' rather than 'I will be confident'.
♦ *Hot words*
  Use words that are meaningful and energising to you.

Read each card at least twice a day. Take 10–20 seconds to do so. As you read it, imagine what you would see, hear and feel when your affirmation becomes real.

7 Supercharging your goal setting

A detailed goal setting process that includes written goals will boost the results you get in life. However, it is also possible to heighten the effects of the process and improve your results.
There are several ways to boost the goal setting process.

(a) Find photographs/pictures that show the observable things that you wish to achieve. This may include a house, a car, or a holiday location. It could also be a picture of you, or someone you love, smiling.
(b) You could draw what you want to achieve. The artistic accuracy is unimportant. The visual representation is important.
(c) You can record your goals and affirmations and play them back to yourself on occasions.

(d) Select specific music that represents a specific goal. Put together short clips of music that represent your key goals and purpose. Each one should be only a minute or two in duration. Play them at least once or twice a day.

By breaking your purpose down into goals that cover several aspects of your life through time, you have created milestones. You are able to see what you intended to achieve over a week or month (or year). As you achieve these smaller goals you can treat them as milestones. They show that you are living 'on purpose' and are moving towards longer term goals.

If you are not arriving at certain milestones, you can ask why. You may identify alternative courses of action or behaviours that will get you back on track, or you may genuinely believe the milestone is no longer important.

A process of regular reviews keeps you focused and action orientated.

So far you have been given the opportunity to improve your self-awareness and your life purpose. If you have diligently applied yourself on these two areas you will make great steps in improving your life. In the next chapter you will be encouraged to improve the way you 'read' other people.

chapter five
empathy – knowing you

Data and Counsellor Troi

In *Star Trek: The Next Generation* there are two characters of interest to us as we are exploring emotional intelligence. One character is the android called Data. He is a highly intelligent member of the crew. He has considerable logical capabilities. However he does not have emotions and he desires them. His emotional limitations cause him to be confused when issues have an emotional content. He often asks childlike, naive questions in an attempt to clarify issues. In one episode of the series Data gets an 'emotions chip' and is overwhelmed by his feelings.

The second character is Counsellor Deanna Troi. She is an 'empath'. Her job requires her to read the emotions of crew members and other parties. Troi can then report what she finds to the captain. She is highly sensitive to picking up and interpreting emotional, non-verbalized information. Outside the world of television research shows that some people resemble Data and others Troi when it comes to reading the emotions of others. The people at the Troi end of the scale fare much better in life. If you are to manage yourself effectively you need to have good empathic skills.

If you are to manage yourself effectively you need to have good empathic skills.

Empathy

A very important component of emotional intelligence is empathy. This is the ability to understand the feelings of others. It is the ability to recognize the concerns of other people. The empathic person is also able to accept the perspective of others. There is value in differentiating between sympathy and empathy as they are sometimes confused. When you feel sympathy you experience what the other person is experiencing. This may be pleasant when the other person is happy, but not so nice when they are distressed. When you feel empathy you understand another's feelings but you do not directly experience them.

Case study

Gary was unable to do his job properly. He was a capable sales manager. Usually he was well organized. His staff loved him. Everyone said Gary was approachable. He was always willing to listen. Indeed, he was considered a very sympathetic person. This resulted in staff being willing to avail themselves of Gary's open door policy. At times staff would talk about many personal issues rather than just work-related problems. This absorbed a large portion of Gary's time. It also resulted in Gary being emotionally burdened by the problems of many staff. This sapped him of energy. It dulled his senses and impaired his decision making.

When a person has good empathic skills they are able to appreciate the differences between people in terms of their emotional responses. Conversely, the absence of this skill means that people are oblivious to important interpersonal signals. The lack of these skills causes a person to appear cold or indifferent. There will usually be complaints that the person is insensitive and does not care.

Empathy is important because many people will not openly communicate important information. They will not say things directly. Instead their feelings must be inferred from other cues (see the sports example below) such as facial expressions, voice tone, posture and rate of speech.

Empathy is important because many people will not openly communicate important information.

In sport empathic skills play a significant role. For coaches, the ability to understand the emotions of the people they are coaching is invaluable. By being able to read whether players are angry, depressed, worried, overexcited or anxious, the coach can decide whether the emotions will interfere with performance and take action. The same applies to captains and team leaders.

When athletes are asked how they feel or whether everything is okay, they tend to be non-committal. The canny coach picks up on all the non-verbal signs and probes further.

Harvard psychologist Robert Rosenthal has conducted extensive research on the subject of empathy. He used a profile of non-verbal sensitivity (PONS) to analyze the levels of empathy of over 7,000 people in 18 countries. The results were consistent across cultures. Those people who scored high on empathy on the PONS were better adjusted emotionally. They were more outgoing and were more popular. In another experiment with over 1,000 children, comparisons were made between children with low and high empathy scores and similar IQs. They found that high empathy children significantly outperformed their low empathy peers.

Getting to know you

As a result of many research programmes, the National Institute of Mental Health in the USA reported that empathic skills are learned in early childhood. They observed that empathic children were disciplined with reference to the emotional impact their behaviour was having on others: 'Look how sad you've made your mother feel', rather than 'that was naughty'. The researchers also found that empathy was learned when children could see how others react when someone else is upset. So, by imitating what they see, young children develop a range of empathic responses.

The ability to know the emotional experiences of others comes from an intimate understanding of oneself (self-awareness). This was highlighted in the innovative research done by Robert Levenson at the University of California. He got married couples to discuss a neutral subject and one that was a source of disagreement. The responses of the couple were recorded in many ways. These included high quality video recordings and heart rate monitors.

Following the recordings, one partner left the psychology laboratory. The other remained and watched the videos. They were asked to narrate on the hidden dialogue of the interactions. What did they feel but not say? Once this has been concluded, the second partner watched the video and said what they thought their partner was feeling and not saying. Levenson was then able to compare the actual feelings with those perceived by the partner.

The partners who were accurate in interpreting the other's emotions exhibited an extraordinary mode of empathic behaviour. It was found that their own body was mimicking their partner's. If the heart rate of their partner rose so did their own. This shows a very high level of empathy.

In other walks of life, such as sales, counselling, teaching and management, the ability to empathize is an important predictor of success. Indeed, recent research in business environments shows that clusters of emotional intelligence skills lead to heightened business performance. Leading experts like Boyatzis have identified that empathy is one of the key skills explaining high performance.

Leading experts like Boyatzis have identified that empathy is one of the key skills explaining high performance.

Case study

Andrea was a highly successful medical sales representative. Like all her colleagues, she had been given a very thorough training. Yet Andrea stood out. Her customers not only bought many of her products, they were exceedingly loyal. Often they would be offered cheaper deals by competitors yet they would stay with Andrea. When Andrea's employers tried to find out why, they identified two qualities. The first was trust. The second was that Andrea always seemed to know how customers were feeling and could sense the customer's mood and respond as required. On reflection, Andrea knew she was responding in this way but could not explain how she did it.

The seven per cent solution

'Mortals can keep no secrets. If their lips are silent, they gossip with their fingertips; betrayal forces its way through every pore.'

Sigmund Freud

So when someone is empathic, what are they doing? What are the unconscious maps that are enabling them to read other people successfully? What are the cues that they are picking up on?

The answers to these and other related questions have been provided by Professor Albert Mehrabian of UCLA. In his groundbreaking research he sought to identify how people communicate with each other. He undertook meticulous studies and came to some startling conclusions. He found that only seven per cent of the total communication came from the specific words and content of the words actually spoken. The other 93 per cent was attributable to other factors. Prominent among these were voice tone, eye movements, physical gestures, posture and related factors. This explains why we sometimes get a 'funny feeling' about what is being said by a person. This is almost certainly because there is an inconsistency between the 7 per cent and the 93 per cent.

Further research by Mehrabian showed that in making our judgements it is the voice tone of the person – its resonance and intonation – that may account for up to 84 per cent of what is being communicated. When judging whether we believe what is being said we tend to rely far more heavily on voice tone than content. Most people have heard someone they know say that they like something and yet doubted their statement. Here they are unconsciously picking up on the non-verbal signals.

Knowing me, knowing you

A second leading researcher in this field has done detailed experiments on the links between emotional states and physiological responses. Paul Elkman has shown that experimental participants who manipulate their facial muscles as he instructed (smiling; frowning, etc) often showed the physiological responses that you might expect. When EEG measures were used, Elkman found that smiling activated those parts of the brain associated with feeling happy. Furthermore, the participants reported that they felt the emotions that were associated with the facial expressions.

When Elkman conducted cross-cultural research, he found that there were universal facial expressions linked with emotional states. Even when Elkman compared isolated pre-literate cultures, like those in Papua New Guinea, with Western countries the same results were found.

This evidence shows that there are hard-wired innate links between emotional states, certain facial muscle movements and autonomic body activity such as heart rate and skin conductance.

The work of Elkman, Mehrabian, Levenson and others shows that there are powerful links between emotions and our physical responses. Those responses are observable. We call people who are good at noticing those responses and interpreting them 'empathic'. There is also evidence that in most people the ability to read these responses is learned early in life. The good news for people who may currently be low on empathy is that they can learn empathic skills. As they do so they can enjoy life more and get better results.

The work of Elkman, Mehrabian, Levenson and others shows that there are powerful links between emotions and our physical responses.

The dark side of empathy

While it is evident that people who score highly on empathy are happier and more successful in their lives, we are left to wonder what happens to people capable of little or no empathy. Not surprisingly, they tend to have few, if any, friends. They have difficulty establishing and maintaining good-quality relationships. However, an absence of empathy may have darker consequences.

Martin Hoffman, a specialist in the psychology of empathy, believes that the roots of our moral behaviour are to be found in empathy. He reasons that the ability to share another person's distress is an essential trigger to helping them. From watching others empathize or reacting themselves, people work out a 'moral system'. They learn which behaviours are right and wrong.

The Hoffman rationale is supported by research done on criminals. It has been established that criminals who are responsible for inflicting some of the most heinous crimes are very low on empathy. They have no appreciation of the way the other person feels. This allows them to behave cruelly and to be oblivious to the suffering they have caused. As a result of this lack of empathy, the criminal has no remorse whatsoever.

Activities

In the activities below, you will be provided with several exercises that will improve your empathic skills. First work through the self-rating scale below. The lower your score the more you need to work on your empathic skills.

1 Where are you now? Self-rating

Score yourself on the scale from 1 to 10 for each statement.

10 = Total agreement

1 = Total disagreement

EMPATHY	SCORE
◆ I am a good listener.	_____
◆ I can put my feelings to one side and appreciate those of others.	_____
◆ I can often detect a person's emotions by their tone of voice.	_____
◆ I can read people's emotions on TV even when the volume is turned down.	_____
◆ I can read between the lines when people are talking.	_____
◆ I can tell when people are upset even if they do not tell me.	_____
◆ I can pick up on the mood of a group when I enter a room.	_____
◆ I can detect people's emotions by observing their body language.	_____
TOTAL	

2 Micro-observations I

To improve your level of empathy it is worthwhile starting by doing some further work on your self-awareness. You have learned that many of our emotional responses are hard-wired into us. So, if you can improve your self-understanding you will be well placed to understand others.

For each emotion listed below, bring to mind your exact response when you experience it. Try looking in a mirror as you do this activity.

If you know how to take your pulse, do so. Notice your facial expressions, posture, rate of breathing and skin tone. As you speak out aloud, notice your rate of speech and your voice tone. You can also make notes when you find yourself spontaneously experiencing an emotion. Alternatively, try and make notes soon after an emotional experience.

Joy
Frustration
Anger
Competitive
Anxious
Fearful
Amused
Once you have worked through these emotional states, begin to work through others.

3 Micro-observations II

Once you have spent time observing yourself, you can begin to focus on other people. Before you look at people that you meet in your daily life, there is a halfway house.

Try selecting films or television programmes that you have not seen, which have a good reputation and high quality actors and actresses. Using a video recorder, tape the show and try working through the following activities.

(a) Run the video for five minutes with no sound. Watch the programme carefully and make notes on what you think is happening. What are the emotions that are on display? You may wish to play through the video clip a few times.

With your notes, run through the clip one more time and reflect upon why you reach the conclusions that you arrive at.

(b) Run other video clips for five minutes each. This time have sound but no visual information. Now try and describe the physical behaviour of performers from what you can hear. Be willing to run through the clip several times.

With your notes, run through the clip one more time and reflect upon why you reach the conclusions that you arrive at.

(c) When you have worked through activities (a) and (b), revisit the clips with full audio-visual information intact. Assess your own accuracy. How well did you do? Where could you improve?

4 Micro-observations III

If you are fortunate enough to have family videos, you can try a similar set of activities to those in Micro-observations II. Your advantage here is that you know the people involved.

5 Micro-observations IV

Once you have worked through the previous three micro-observation activities, you are ready to go native. You can build up your skills gradually. Don't rush. A few minutes a day done consistently will soon bring improvements.

(a) Select a few people that you know. They may be at home, at work or people you meet in other walks of life.

(b) For a few minutes, observe a person. Notice how they communicate. Be aware of verbal and non-verbal cues. What do you notice? How does it help you to understand what is being communicated?

(c) Where possible, encourage people you have observed to discuss their emotions at a time when you were watching them. Check out whether you were accurate.

6 Micro-observations V

In this exercise you are encouraged to focus upon single non-verbal cues to explain what emotions are being experienced at the time. First make observations of yourself and then observe others (either on video or in person).

Start by making observations on the following:

◆ Times when the rate of breathing quickens.
◆ Times when your voice tone changes.
◆ Times when your skin tone reddens.
◆ Times when your throat tightens.
◆ Times when you may perspire (with no increase in external temperature).

Once you have worked through these non-verbal cues, select and work through others.

7 Empathy

As you become more experienced using all the micro-observations, start to work through the emotions you have observed.

Make notes on the physical, non-verbal cues that lead you to identify a certain emotion. Also consider the way each emotion influences the way people analyze, synthesize and make decisions.

8 Perceptual positions

A great way to develop your empathy skills is to use a technique called 'perceptual positions'. Basically, when you are interacting with another person it is possible to look at the situation from several perspectives. These perspectives include:

◆ your own – self
◆ through the eyes of the other person involved – other

◆ through the eyes of a neutral observer – neutral

Each perspective is a perceptual position. By getting into the habit of seeing things from all three perspectives you will be able to develop your empathic skills. When you find yourself in an interaction, try out the ideas described below.

◆ *Self*
Be aware of what you see, hear and feel. This focuses upon self-awareness. You may ask yourself: What do I feel now? What do I desire now?

◆ *Other*
Put yourself in the other's shoes. What precisely can they see, hear and feel? What impressions are they picking up? How will the behaviour of others make them feel?

◆ *Neutral*
Put yourself into the position of the observer. How are the two people interacting? How do they influence each other?

People who are able to move around the perceptual positions have a wider perspective. This gives them more choices and a greater capacity to get positive results. The perceptual positions allow you to appreciate the perspective of other people. It allows you to see yourself as others see you. Finally, a detached view enables you to see how behaviours interact.

A manager may not delegate because she feels that a member of staff has very low motivation. At the same time the member of staff is demotivated because he is not given additional responsibilities. Unless these two people can explore alternative positions they will each be stuck – understandably – in a sub-optimal state.

Take a moment to think about important relationships in your life that may be 'stuck'. Try working through the three perceptual positions and explore whether this can get you out of the stuck state.

Your ability to empathize was learned as a child. It is probably such a well established 'map' that you do not question it. You take it as a fixed aspect of your life. If you are empathic then this is okay. However if you are weak in this area you can do something about it. By doing these exercises you can relearn your empathic capabilities and improve the quality of your life.

06

chapter six
intuition – magical feelings

Spock v. Kirk

In many of the original *Star Trek* episodes there were scenes where the views of Captain Kirk and Mr Spock came into conflict. Few would doubt that Spock was more intelligent than his senior officer. His grasp of science and his powers of logic were vastly superior to Kirk's. At times this was his strength. He could make calculations and draw rational and logical conclusions. However, at other times Spock was flummoxed – though he never put it that way. He would look quizzical and say that something or other was not logical.

This is why Kirk had an advantage over Spock. At times he would listen to Spock's advice and benefit from it. Yet there were times when the observable data and logic were not enough. With imminent disaster facing the crew of the *Enterprise*, the saving of the day may need more than a perplexed look and the advice 'it's not logical'. Yet, nestled between Spock's logic and Dr McCoy having a panic attack ('For God's sake, Jim, do something!'), Captain James T. Kirk would take action. Here he responded to 'a hunch', his 'gut feeling', his instinct. It is this instinctive or intuitive response that gave Kirk the edge. Both Spock and McCoy may have scored higher in IQ tests. However, it was Kirk's EI and his intuition that saved the day.

Einstein's Insight

It may be one thing to take a quick look at *Star Trek*, but does this stuff have any relevance to real world activities? The answer is a firm 'yes'. Furthermore, there is a mass of intriguing scientific evidence to support the notion of intuition – as we will see later in this chapter.

The whole area of scientific research, in all subjects, is thought of as being highly rational and logical. This view is personified by Mr Spock. The focus is on the observable. It is on measurement and drawing logical solutions. There is an air of clinical, emotionless calculation. Yet this could not be further from the truth. All the logical and rational elements are important. Indeed it is possible to be an adequate 'jobbing' scientist using these skills. However, a closer look at scientists shows there to be important emotional intelligences in play. These include the goal orientation to answer the most challenging questions. There is the emotional management skills to persist despite setbacks. For all breakthroughs there is creativity and innovation. And there is the role of intuition.

Albert Einstein is still regarded as the greatest scientist of modern times. He is seen as an eccentric man with a powerful scientific intellect (both are true). Einstein himself wrote 'The really valuable thing is intuition'. Another eminent quantum physicist, Max Planck, firmly believed that 'a vivid intuitive imagination for new ideas not generated by deduction' was essential for the scientist.

These are not exceptions. They are much more typical of the views of scientists. Whether it is coming up with large scientific breakthroughs or solving a small problem, the baseline is their technical knowledge plus 'a hunch'. So even in the world of science, where we might expect logic and rational analysis to be supreme, there is a key role for intuition. There is little doubt that intuition is often a valued skill in sport.

One of the most valuable emotional intelligence qualities in sport, too is intuition. The vocabulary of many sports is peppered with references to intuitive capabilities. It is widely recognized that these capabilities give the competitor the edge. For example, in tennis we often hear of players playing instinctive shots. They would not have time to make logical decisions. They must simply react. Some tennis players have an uncanny ability to 'guess right'. This skill is often called anticipation and it is valued in the game.

Likewise, when coaches are asked why they made certain tactical choices they attribute them to gut feelings. A similar explanation is given when athletes are asked why they play a certain shot, run to a certain position on the field or make the choices they do. More often than not it is a decision based on a hunch or instinct.

What CEOs really feel

The world of business is one where considerable emphasis is placed upon rational analysis. This commitment to measurement and the creation of logical decision making models has, in part, accounted for success in the marketplace. Yet even here, in an environment of the measurable and the observable, there is a role for intuitions. When Harvard Professor Henry Mintzberg looked at the chief executive officers at the USA's leading companies he made a startling finding, which was reported in the *Harvard Business Review*. It was clear that the best managers were 'holistic thinkers' who were constantly relying on hunches to deal with problems far too complex for rational analysis. He wrote that 'Organizational effectiveness does not lie in that narrow-minded concept called 'rationality'; it lies in a blend of clear-headed logic and powerful intuition.' A recent article in *The Sunday Times* illustrates this use of intuition.

The Sunday Times on March 24th 2002 carried a feature on the Chief Executive Officer of the sportswear giant Adidas. The title of the article was 'Instinct Scores for Adidas Boss'.

The opening paragraph captured the key points in the article:

'Should businessmen make decisions based on gut instinct? Some tycoons swear by it, while traditionalists prefer the tried-and-tested techniques of management schools. In reality the best managers probably dabble with both.'

The Adidas CEO, Herbert Hainer, is quoted in the article as saying, 'I can smell good and bad decisions . . . It is in my blood and I feel it in my stomach.'

The article concluded with Hainer adding:

'I probably err more on the side of formal business processes, but when you take decisions every day you can't always draw up a business plan. My natural feelings always help and I feel my way through deals.'

The use of intuition is logical!

The use of intuition is logical! In many business situations decision makers are confronted with situations where:

◆ they must act on partial information

◆ they are bombarded with highly complex information and little time to make a full logical analysis

◆ nobody has the 'right' answer as it is a new area of business.

Add to this the fact that our brains can only hold 7 ± 2 chunks of information in the conscious mind at any one time. So if we have to 'get our heads around' 10 or more items we can't easily do it. In such circumstances managers still need to make decisions and take action. Many of the most successful managers, like Mintzberg's cohort, trust their intuition.

The uses of intuition

Such is the recognition of the importance of intuition that there have been many studies attempting to explore further how intuition can be broken down into key components and how managers use intuition. The work of two leading researchers are summarized below.

Professor Daniel Isenberg (from Harvard)

Managers use intuition to:

- help them sense when a problem exists
- rapidly perform well learned behaviour patterns
- synthesize isolated bits of data and experience into an integrated picture
- check the results of rational analysis – matching it with gut feeling.

Professor George Turin (from Berkeley)

The intuitive components are:

- the ability to know how to attack a problem without knowing how you know
- the ability to relate problems in one field to those in unrelated fields – seeing new links and connections
- the ability to recognize the crux of a problem
- the ability to see in advance a general solution to a problem
- the ability to recognize solutions because they feel right.

You and your intuition

'The intuitive mind is a sacred gift and the rational mind is a faithful servant. We have created a society that honours the servant and has forgotten the gift.'

Albert Einstein

The challenge of partial information, limited time and new areas of activity are not the exclusive domain of business managers. They apply to everyone in their daily life. Often there is a tendency to try and apply an old solution. Sometimes they work but sometimes they do not. Indeed, people will often try an old approach that they know failed. They simply 'hope' it will work the next time.

There are many times when we have hunches and we ignore them.

There are many times when we have hunches and we ignore them. We find ourselves saying things like 'I knew I should not have done that!', 'I had a bad feeling about him from the start (yet I went ahead).', 'Something was telling me to say no (yet out of habit I said yes)'. These are all examples of our intuitions giving us a message that, for some reason, we ignore. Likewise, we often make spontaneous choices that come good. The scenarios below are typical examples of the role of intuition, and its absence, in business.

Case study

Connie was committed to taking a measured and detailed approach to work. She had trained as an accountant. She had an excellent reputation as an auditor and had proven proficient as a user of planning models. When she became a manager she wanted to apply the same rigour to her job. This proved increasingly problematic. Connie was keen to try and use time consuming approaches when quick decisions were needed. She just could not cope with acting on instinct. In fast-moving situations Connie found it hard to make decisions and manage others.

Ron is an exceptional entrepreneur. When he started his business he did not have the money for detailed market research. He simply had a hunch that people would be willing to buy financial services in new ways. He was right. Throughout his career Ron has used phrases like 'This feels right', 'My head says yes but my heart says no', 'I just feel it in my gut'. Even as a highly successful businessman, he listens to his instincts as to who to trust and where the market is going. His success is a tribute that this approach works. He uses proper systems and methodologies. Yet Ron knows that this is not enough. When asked to explain it he simply shrugs his shoulders and answers, 'I can't.'

Trusting your hunches

'You have to leave the city of your comfort and go into the wilderness of your intuition. What you'll discover will be wonderful. What you'll discover will be yourself.'

Alan Alda

So far you have seen that in the fields of science and business there is an important role for intuition. You may be able to recall times when trusting or not trusting your hunches has had an impact on the quality of your life. There is also further scientific evidence that should encourage you to work on your intuitive capabilities.

Professor Candace Pert

Early research on emotions had shown that the flow of emotions and thoughts started, always, in the brain. More recently, Pert and others have shown that the flow starts from many sites in the body. The sites include the immune, nervous, endocrine and gastro-intestinal systems. In this way intelligence is diffused throughout the body. Many neuropeptides – the building blocks of intelligence – originate in the gut. No wonder we use gut reactions to make intelligent decisions.

No wonder we use gut reactions to make intelligent decisions.

Institute of Heartmath

The Institute of Heartmath has undertaken research on the impact of the heart on people's thinking, feeling and deciding. The heart beats at least 110,000 times a day. It has significant electromagnetic, neuronal and hormonal properties.

The significance of our hearts is reflected in our day-to-day language. Phrases such as 'big hearted', 'cold heart' and 'heart in mouth' are but a few examples.

The Institute shows that the electrical impact of the heart on the body is 40–60 that of the brain. The researchers show that the heart's electromagnetic signals are transmitted to every cell of the body. Indeed, the signals can be measured up to five feet away from a person. The Institute has shown that the body (heart) influences the brain.

Skin conductance responses (SCR)

Researchers have found that when our thoughts change it leads to changes in emotions. This then leads to changes in our nervous system. While many of the changes are unobservable to the naked eye, they can be picked up on polygraph machines. The greater the emotional changes the greater the size of the waves on the polygraph machine.

Professor Damasio has conducted many experiments using SCR. He has shown that people have 'Anticipatory Psychophysical Responses' prior to making conscious decisions. They have 'gut feelings' or 'instincts' before they begin rational thinking. He has also shown that at times we have emotional responses that we are not conscious of, yet they still influence our decisions.

This diverse academic research is very detailed. It is based upon biological and physical experimentation. All of it indicates that there are powerful things going on at the subconscious level. Our entire bodies have intellectual capabilities, our hearts exert an influence on our thinking and feeling and it is possible to process information subconsciously before we ever become aware of it. The hard science and our own experiences suggest that we have physical sources of information (intuitive intelligence) that can supplement our conventional rational thinking processes. If you want to manage yourself effectively then it makes sense to tune in to this powerful source of intelligence. You can learn to utilize your intuition. Let's have a look at how you may do this.

chapter six

managing yourself

momentum

If you want to manage yourself effectively then it makes sense to tune in to this powerful source of intelligence.

Activities

The activities described below are designed to help you to develop your intuitive skills. First work through the self-rating scale below. The lower your score the more you need to work on your intuition. The aim is to work on the activities and enjoy doing so.

---

1 Where are you now? Self-rating

Score yourself on the scale from 1 to 10 for each statement.

10 = Total agreement
1 = Total disagreement

INTUITION	SCORE
◆ I believe in using intuition every time.	_____
◆ Sometimes I get to the right answer without clear reasons.	_____
◆ My gut reaction is usually right.	_____
◆ I sometimes sense who is calling me before I answer the telephone.	_____
◆ When faced with tough decisions I trust my hunches.	_____
◆ Sometimes I let my heart rule my head.	_____
◆ My feelings are often more accurate than my reason.	_____
◆ Using intuition is a valuable part of my life.	_____
TOTAL	☐

The role of silence

'True silence is the rest of the mind. It is to the spirit what sleep is to the body, nourishment and refreshment.'

Williams Penn

One of the most valuable things in life is silence. The levels and numbers of sounds are constantly on the increase. There is excellent scientific evidence to show that meditation in an environment of silence leads to people being psychologically happier and physically healthier. As our conscious mind gets distracted by external noises we may fail to notice our internal messages (or intuitions). By consciously seeking silence we open ourselves up to our intuitions.

2 Time out and silence

Many people find it very difficult to deal with silence. Even sitting in silence for a couple of minutes is a challenge. The constant noise and running commentary of thoughts means that feelings and intuitions get blocked out.

So, be willing to take a pause of a few seconds when having conversations or making decisions. Aim to notice your hunches in the silence.

Each day identify times when there may be silence and resist the temptation to 'fill the gap' with music, radio, television or idle conversation. Instead, allow yourself to notice any intuitions you may be having.

3 Silent minutes

Try taking 3–5 minutes at the start and end of each day. Notice your thoughts and how you feel. Then go a little further and notice your gut feelings and intuitions. Make a written note of what you experience.

Practice intuitions

The next four exercises are all designed to open up your mind to your intuitions. Some of you will already be doing these things. If you are not, just try them. With time you will achieve unconscious competence in letting intuitions play a role.

4 Ask yourself intuitions questions

We are used to asking ourselves analytical and rational questions. It is also possible to ask our intuitive self clear questions. Typical questions would be, 'How do I feel about this challenge?', or 'What is my hunch about this option?'. A willingness to ask these questions and notice the answers that come will open you up to your intuition.

5 Notice your first response

In your day-to-day activities you will be asking your intuitive self questions. It is important to notice your immediate response. There will often be plenty of old ideas and critical thoughts so check you are noting the first intuitive response.

6 How are you intuitive?

When you experience intuitions ask yourself: What exactly am I experiencing? Where is it? What is it? How does it feel?

7 Develop insight

There is a myth that people who develop their intuitions jettison their analytical thinking. This is not so. Begin to notice the interplay between your instincts and your analysis.

8 Intuitive anticipation

The following scenarios encourage you to anticipate events and to trust your intuitions.

(a) When the telephone rings, prior to answering, ask yourself the following:

- Is the call for you/another person?
- Is the caller male/female?
- Is it local/long distance?

(b) Before the mail arrives, ask yourself:

- How much will come?
- How many bills will come?
- How much junk mail will come?

(c) Before a meeting, ask yourself:

- What will be the mood of the other people who will be there?
- How will people be dressed?
- Who will be constructive/destructive?

(d) Other options

Select other situations and events where you can test your ability to anticipate what will happen.

For all these anticipatory activities try and keep a note of your responses.

Let your body talk to you

Kinesiology

Everything we have looked at in this chapter has focused upon your willingness to listen to your body; to your intuitions. In the next exercise you will be given a technique for asking your body direct questions and getting answers! There is a branch of scientific enquiry called Kinesiology. It has created a technique called muscle testing. The testing allows you to communicate with your body. You should work with a friend and give it a try.

9 Muscle testing

Choose a friend for testing. We'll call them your subject.

(a) Have the subject stand erect, right arm relaxed at their side, left arm held out parallel to the floor, elbow straight.

(b) Face the subject and place your left hand on their right shoulder to steady them. Then place your right hand on the subject's extended left arm just above the wrist.

(c) Tell the subject you are going to try to push the arm down as they resist with all their strength.

(d) Now push down on the arm fairly quickly, firmly and evenly. The idea is to push just hard enough to test the spring and bounce in the arm, not so hard that the muscle becomes fatigued. It is not a question of who is stronger, but of whether the muscle can 'lock' the shoulder joint against the push.

(Do not smile when you are conducting this test or when you are being tested yourself.)

(e) Unless there is some physical problem with the muscle, it will test strong. Assuming it does, give your subject a little refined sugar to eat and test again. In nearly every case, the muscle will now test weak; although you are pushing down no harder than before, the muscle will not be able to resist the pressure and the subject's arm will fall to the side.

(f) Practice muscle testing by exploring responses to foods such as:
- **(i)** tea
- **(ii)** water
- **(iii)** fish
- **(iv)** cheese

(g) Explore responses to thoughts of the following daily situations:
- **(i)** winning
- **(ii)** losing

(iii) struggling

(iv) conflict

(h) Now allow your friend to muscle test you.

(i) Choose your own example foods and thoughts.

The muscle test provides a direct line to the body and measures a pure physical response. With time you will be able to map out strengthening/weakening scenarios by getting answers straight from the body.

This exercise shows us that at a deeper, instinctive level our body is responding and now you can tap into that.

By using these exercises you can make substantial improvements in your use of intuition. This will improve the quality and speed of your decisions in every walk of life.

chapter seven
integrity: you can't fake it

Developing trust and integrity

'Technique and technology are important. But adding trust is the issue of the decade.'

Tom Peters

Very few people have successful and high quality lives in total isolation. In some artistic pursuits it is possible to be a comparable loner. However, in most cases it helps to work well with other people.

To work effectively with other people it is important to develop trusting relationships. It is necessary to be able to communicate well and to create good team working environments. To be able to do all these things requires a series of competencies that can be called social skills. When you possess these skills you are able to move more quickly towards your goals.

Case study

Shakira was an experienced life coach. She had established a reputation for helping people to overcome obstacles in their life. Initially she had worked on a face-to-face basis. As her reputation grew, the demand for her services expanded throughout the country. This led Shakira to offering telephone coaching. She was also highly successful here. The growth of online services led Shakira into offering online coaching. This was done through a combination of e-mails and 'chat room' real time exchanges. When the results were evaluated it became obvious to Shakira that the online approach was slower and less effective in many cases.

In an electrical goods company there were several assembly units. A new product was introduced and it required new ways of working and slightly different skills. The product was introduced at two separate sites. The same methods of training and working were utilized. After a couple of months the assembly lines were evaluated. There were significant differences in terms of productivity and quality. When the reasons for this variation were sought the answer proved elusive. The competence experience of staff in both places was virtually identical. The past record of both places was comparable and the implementation of the new work methods had been done in an identical way.

Further research identified one 'cultural' difference between the two sites. In the productive site there was an atmosphere of trust. The senior managers were respected for their honesty and integrity. However, at the second site there was an atmosphere of suspicion. The staff did not think that their managers were liars. They just did not feel that there was any openness. There was a sense of things being 'held back'.

The trust issue was critical. Where it existed, the staff would be open about difficulties and they would share solutions. Where trust was missing, people tended to 'cover their backs'. They would not be open about problems and this led to productivity and quality problems. There was an unwillingness to share information. People withheld good ideas.

There is a whole training and development industry that has emerged around subjects such as social skills and communications skills. Their approach is useful. However, at times it can be superficial or darn right manipulative.

In this chapter I will provide you with a brief introduction to the traditional social skills training. Then I want to suggest a different approach; one that puts deeper values, such as trust and integrity, first.

Rapport and traditional approaches

One of the most popular social skills topics is rapport. This is the sense of strong interpersonal connection between people. Conventional training aims to help people to quickly develop rapport with others. In this way others will like you, trust you and act upon your suggestions. This deep, non-verbal contact is supplemented by other 'trust building techniques'. One example that illustrates the social skills mindset is called the 'Yes set'.

Mirroring and matching

The most popular way to create rapport is to use mirroring and matching. This technique copies a naturally occurring process. When you observe two people who are in love you will see that their movements almost copy each other's. They often 'finish each other's sentences'.

When it is taught, the student is encouraged to mirror the movements and behaviour of the person with whom they are communicating. If they are seated opposite a person and the person moves their left hand, then the student subtly moves their right hand. If the head is tilted to the right, the student tilts their head to the left. In this way a person is almost seeing a reflection of themselves in the student.

This process is developed in ever greater detail. So the student will notice the rate and depth of breathing of the subject. They will notice the movement of the diaphragm and match it. As the breathing is matched it makes it easier to match the rates of speaking.

The matching process is extended to the speech patterns being used by the subject. So the words and sentence structure is also matched. If the subject expresses themselves in a certain way then the student states their ideas using the language of the subject.

When all the mirroring and matching techniques are combined they are very powerful. The subject is being 'hit' at many non-verbal levels by congruent communications. This is the 93 per cent of communication identified by Mehrabian. When the subject senses that the person that they are speaking to is like them then they are more likely to trust them. They are more likely to suspend their critical faculties and act 'on trust'.

The Yes Set

The user of the Yes Set has a very simple aim. They want to get the person they are with to get into the habit of answering yes to several questions. This is done by asking simple questions where the answer is obviously going to be 'yes', such as:

'It is a sunny day?'
'You got here on time?'
'You are drinking tea today?'

As the person answers yes to these and other questions they experience the comfort of being known and feel more relaxed. The essence is to start with the question that it is easiest to answer 'yes' to. This builds a climate of agreement. Soon there is a habit of agreement. The more people agree the more they are likely to continue agreeing.

The micro-agreements that arise out of the Yes Set lead to a willingness to agree on less superficial issues. The subject who keeps answering yes has an ever deeper sense of being understood. They believe that the questioner shares their view of the world. When people are taught Yes Set techniques they will be told something along the lines of:

'When a customer has said 'yes' throughout the presentation, it is very hard for him to say 'no' at the close.'

D. Moine & K. Lloyd

There is a sophisticated collection of techniques that may be combined to provide managers, salespeople and others with potentially manipulative social skills. They can be combined with many of the persuasion techniques that have been brilliantly summarized by Cialdini, a Professor at Arizona State University and author of *Influence* (see box below). This whole chapter on social skills could be dedicated to presenting these techniques. Indeed, there are whole books on the subject. However, there is a different way of looking at social skills; one that works at a genuinely deeper level; one that replaces the outward appearance of trust and integrity with . . . (fanfare, please) . . . actual trust and integrity!

Psychological Gimmicks (as identified by Cialdini)

Here are a few examples of techniques that are used to 'persuade' people to do something.

1 *Reciprocation.* First a favour is provided. This is often a small gift or 'act of kindness'. It then becomes difficult to say no to a request from the giver. Certain religious groups give you a free flower and ask for a donation. This brings in more money than 'selling' the flowers.

2 *Puppy dog.* The potential buyer is given a free trial. This is a gift and it gets the person to live with the product/service. Once again, it makes it difficult to give back the 'puppy'.

3 *Concession and contrast.* First a person is shown something suitable but very highly priced. Then an alternative is presented at a lower price. This option seems eminently reasonable.

4 *Impending events.* A sense of urgency is created about the purchase or action. A decision is needed against a deadline 'as there are three other people who want this one product'.

Before exploring integrity and trust in a little more depth, it is worth discovering how communications and interactions can be differentiated into three distinct levels.

Three levels of communication and social skills

There are several organizations, like the Institute of Heartmath, which have identified different levels of communication. By understanding how these levels operate, we are able to develop our social skills much more deeply. It is possible to differentiate three levels. They are linked and influence each other. The levels are surface, feeling and core.

By understanding how these levels operate, we are able to develop our social skills much more deeply.

Surface level

Here the focus is upon what is being said and some simple observable non-verbal signals. The person sending the message tends to concentrate on the words they are using. When the receiver does the same there is still considerable scope for confusion. There may be a misinterpretation of words. It is possible for people who are poor with words to get themselves into difficulties. In surface level work the tip of the iceberg is studied at the expense of everything else.

Much of the conventional training and development on social skills is delivered at this level. This training often ignores the other two levels. This can result in the training appearing manipulative. There is a tendency to see the techniques as ways of getting your own way, rather than building meaningful relationships.

Feeling level

It is possible to probe below the surface level, to recognize words and gestures and then seek a still deeper level of connection and understanding. At this level our interactions are influenced by our self-awareness, our intuitions and our empathic skills.

At the feeling level you are tapping into your own deeper responses and looking for the deeper meaning being communicated by other people.

Core level

The third and deepest level may be called the core level. This level is tapped into when we are able to define our deepest purpose, our most important values. Once we have tapped into this core part of our being we can then try and communicate in a way that is consistent with it. Likewise, we can try to understand the communication and behaviours of others in terms of all three levels. So you may hear what someone is saying (surface) and ask whether it is consistent with their feelings and their core.

When our social relationships are conducted at a surface level it is possible that the surface communication is inconsistent with the deeper levels. This is incongruous and is perceived as such by others. People with good empathic skills will pick up on these inconsistencies.

However, if our social relationships are driven – bottom up – by our core values then we cannot help being congruent. As our core is at the heart of our communications it will influence our feelings and then our surface level behaviour.

As our core is at the heart of our communications it will influence our feelings and then our surface level behaviour.

Experiencing the levels

Anecdotally, we experience these levels in our day-to-day lives. At the extreme end we may meet people who have slick verbal and presentation skills yet we simply do not trust them. Somehow (empathy/intuition) we know that they lack integrity. Conversely, there are people who are tongue tied or verbally limited yet we trust them implicitly. We connect with these people at a deeper level. They may have difficulty getting their message across. However, we are patient and are happy to work with these authentic people.

The heart of social skills: integrity

Rather than look at basic skills, it is possible to look at human relationships at a deeper and more mature level. By connecting with people at this level you can create genuinely meaningful relationships – at the core.

Professor David Kolb, a leading expert on learning models and Chairman of Organizational Behaviour at Case Western University, described integrity as the highest form of human intelligence. He believes that it is a deep state of consciousness. It pulls together creativity, intuition and rational capacities.

Core characteristics of integrity

There are three central elements to personal integrity. When they are combined and people act in this way then there is a sense of integrity.

1   *Discernment*. There is a degree of moral reflectiveness. Here there is a questioning of whether things are right or wrong.

2   *Action*. The discerned upon issues are then subject to actions. Here people are willing to take actions that are consistent with their 'moral' values. There are outward and visible signs of what a person believes. Sometimes this is clear because the person is making 'a stand'. At times, this action will incur risks. There may be others who oppose the action and take oppositional actions themselves.

3   *Openness*. Making it clear and explaining the source of your actions.

In life it is worth remembering that there is an interesting relationship between integrity and honesty. For example, you may be brutally honest with a friend. So brutal that they are hurt. With a little thought, alternative behaviours could have been selected. These would not have been lies but the alternatives would not have hurt your friend. Likewise, a racist may be honest in stating their racism yet they would not be thought of as possessing integrity.

So integrity has a genuine consideration of the needs of other people. It is a recognition of the deep (core) value of every person, even if they hold different opinions to yourself.

So integrity has a genuine consideration of the needs of other people.

Integrity in others

When someone has a clear set of core values (discernment) they act consistently with these values (action) and express why they do as they do (openness). They are seen to have personal integrity. It is possible that you may not share this person's values. But at least everything is above board and clear. You know where you stand with such a person. You are also able to predict their responses and behaviours. This is because you know their values and that they are consistent.

Even in an environment where there may be some disagreements, it is possible to have a trusting relationship with a high integrity person.

Even in an environment where there may be some disagreements, it is possible to have a trusting relationship with a high integrity person. If they have good ethics then you know that backstabbing or manipulation is off the agenda. This background makes it easier for people to share information and take risks.

Fairness and trust

'You may be deceived if you trust too much, but you will live in torment if you don't trust enough.'

Frank Crane

One of the most influential factors when creating trusting relationships is that of fairness. If people believe that they are treated unfairly then they are less inclined to be trusting. Would you think that someone who had treated you unfairly was trustworthy? Probably not.

For most people fairness does not mean that they get preferential treatment. It is simply a desire that people are treated appropriately. To do this well implies that people clearly understand what is required of them and what the rewards will be. Huseman and

Hatfield, authors of *Managing the Equity Factor* (1989), researched how people respond when they feel that they are giving more than they take; when they feel that they are being treated unfairly. Broadly, they feel distressed and will respond in one of three ways:

1 They reduce inputs. They cut their contributions to their personal and work relationships. They withhold information. They arrive late and leave early. Their outputs are careless and error strewn. There is forgetfulness, absenteeism and, at times, sabotage.

2 They increase outcomes. They try to change what they get from personal and work relationships. The demand rises, promotions and bonuses. They look for enhanced status, holidays and job security.

3 They exit. They are unhappy with the unfairness and decide to remove themselves from the situation completely.

In these circumstances it is possible to redress the balance of fairness. This is done by taking time to learn more about the distressed people. What do the unhappy people truly value? What do they want at a deeper level? With this knowledge it may then be possible to treat the person more fairly and build trust.

This illustrates the need to move from the surface level to the core. If you see someone being careless and tardy, or observe someone being demanding, then it is possible to be irritated by this behaviour. If this happens, then you are in danger of responding negatively to the 'ungrateful' person. However, by trying to get to a person's core level it may be possible to resolve problems. With deeper understanding it is possible to explore alternative options. Also, the very effort to understand people at a deeper level can itself redress the balance.

The level of trust between people will have a significant impact on their relationship and organizational efficiency at a time of change. When there is a lack of trust people will be suspicious. They will withhold information, be unwilling to take risks and will dedicate time and energy to 'covering their backs'. All this activity poisons relations and wastes resources. Conversely, where trust exists people pull together when challenged. They share with each other. They support each other. This leads to a better quality of life and more efficient organizations.

Deeper listening

When interacting with other people and developing relationships it is possible to listen in ways that go below the surface level. When seeking to listen at a deeper level there are certain things that you should try to do.

1 Allow a few seconds of silence. Get in touch with your core level. Then recognize that the person you are speaking to also has a core level.

2 Try and feel a sense of appreciation for the other person as an individual. They are more than the words they are speaking at that moment in time.

3 Allow the person the opportunity to state their views without interruptions or judgement.

4 In the time you are with that person, give them your undivided attention. Do not have your mind elsewhere.

5 Patiently attempt to move from surface to core levels.

6 Resist the desire to respond defensively. Be willing to judge feedback openly.

This approach helps the person you are seeking to understand. Often you will end up helping them to clarify their thinking. At times the person realizes that they are incongruent. They may be behaving in ways at a surface level that, on reflection, take them way from their core values. Conversely, the person may be consistent. There may be very real differences of substance. However, a deeper, respectful level of understanding will still help the relationship.

Heartmapping

A further illustration of the desire to work at a deeper level comes from the Institute of Heartmath (see the box below). Here they have gone beyond the logical analysis of a problem; how to improve teamwork. They have gone to the feeling and core levels to look for answers.

From chaos to coherence: improving teamwork by Doc Childre and Bruce Cryer

Mindmapping results

◆ Have effective leadership.

◆ Establish common goals, identifying targets, timetables and sense of urgency.

◆ Ensure correct composition and diversity of team members.

◆ Assign specific responsibilities to team members.

◆ Pay attention to building teams.

◆ Identify resources available to teams.

◆ Run meetings better.

◆ Improve communication.

◆ Identify key information for sharing.

◆ Establish rewards and incentives for all team members.

◆ Identify win-win solutions.

◆ Be competent, have clarity.

◆ Trust team members.

- Deliver results.

- Celebrate success and have fun.

The same people were then asked to produce a heartmap whereby they were encouraged to think with their hearts rather than minds . . .

Heartmapping

- Promote friendship and camaraderie.

- Place higher importance on appreciation of understanding.

- Help each other using interindividual coaching.

- Promote a sense of togetherness.

- Learn and evolve together.

- Promote harmony.

- Reward openness.

- Pay attention to 'team chemistry'.

- Celebrate more often and put greater value on a 'positive atmosphere'.

- Identify and work from the 'team's spirit and soul'.

The heartmapping research provides some excellent ideas for improving teamwork. It also shows the virtue of digging deeper. There are very real contributions to be made by considering feelings and core values. This does not mean that surface level operations and traditional thinking are redundant. Rather, it is possible to develop other ways of operating.

Whether it be listening, generating ideas or improving teams, it is evident that a deeper approach to social skills is valuable. The bottom line is; how do you want to live your life? You may choose to operate at a surface level where you are withholding and assume everyone else is behaving in a similar way. Or you choose integrity and trust. The choice is yours.

The bottom line is; how do you want to live your life?

We rarely take time to look at our moral compass and our behaviour. I now want to encourage you to do so. The exercises and activities that follow provide such an opportunity. Take it!

Activities

The ability to develop trusting relationships contributes to the quality of our lives and our ability to get things done. It is yet another aspect of emotional intelligence that you can measurably improve. Start by working through the self-rating exercise. The lower your score the more you need to do here. Try out the exercises and notice the impact they have on your quality of life.

---

1 Where are you now? Self-rating

Score yourself on the scale from 1 to 10 for each statement.

10 = Total agreement
1 = Total disagreement

SELF-AWARENESS	SCORE
◆ I regularly ask open questions.	_____
◆ I am able to listen attentively.	_____
◆ I frequently develop rapport with people I have just met.	_____
◆ I admit it when I make a mistake.	_____
◆ I can connect with people at a deeper level.	_____
◆ My word is my bond.	_____
◆ I tell the truth even at difficult times.	_____
◆ I do not tell lies.	_____
TOTAL	

▶

2 Circle of trust

The circle of trust technique provides a great way to start thinking about the issue of trust. You have the opportunity to look at yourself and the world you experience. This allows you to understand yourself better.

(a) Imagine yourself surrounded by a circle of trust. Make a list of the family, colleagues, friends, etc. who are inside your trust circle. It may help to draw a diagram and write the names on it.

(b) Reflect upon how people get into your circle. What causes you to expel someone from your circle of trust?

(c) Try asking other people if you are inside their circle of trust. Ask people to explain why you are in their circle or outside it.

In the next exercise you can develop your understanding of trust further.

3 Creating your trust balance sheet

This exercise provides a framework for looking at your day-to-day actions. The things you actually do and how they influence the people around you. The trust balance sheet also gives you an easy-to-use technique for managing your trustworthiness each and every day.

For the people close to you in life, imagine that you have a trust balance sheet with credits and debits (see the example below). You can make some notes on the balance sheet or create your own. Are you in credit/debit?

TRUST BALANCE SHEET

Debit (withdrawals)	Credit (deposits)
Small examples	*Small examples*
◆ sarcasm	◆ smiling
◆ indifference	◆ showing an interest
Large examples	*Large examples*
◆ insults	◆ generous praise
◆ questioning their honesty	◆ trusting them with responsibility

Select two important people in your life. For a week, concentrate on increasing the genuine deposits you make in the balance sheet. Make a list of the things you can do – and do them!

After your week's trial, reflect upon your activities. How did people respond? How did you feel about making this effort? What else could you do to build trust?

As you get into the habit of recording more and more trust balance sheets you will be able to move on to the next exercise.

4 Trust balance sheet debits

When you have worked through several trust balance sheets, take a look back at them. Are there any behaviours that seem to lead to withdrawals on more than one balance sheet? Can you identify those aspects of your behaviour that seem to undermine your trustworthiness? If you are feeling brave, you can put this last question directly to other people. When you have your answer, take action to remove the source of the debits.

This is a very challenging exercise. The trick is to compile several balance sheets first, and to do so without doing any comparisons. Then, when you collate all the information, it is possible that some powerful patterns will emerge. These patterns may be the unconscious maps that drive your life without you knowing it. The patterns may be having a significant impact on your relationships without you appreciating it. Whenever these patterns undermine a person's ability to trust you − change them!

5 Where do you stand?

The 'Where do you stand?' exercise comprises of five simple questions. While simple, they seek to go to your core. They seek to help you discover your moral compass. This will guide you in your day-to-day activities. It should also be consistent with your purpose. Ask yourself the following questions − and make sure you answer them honestly:

◆ What do I stand for?
◆ Do I consciously discern what is right and what is wrong, act on what I believe is right and explain my action openly?
◆ What do I hope for in my collaborations with others?
◆ What am I willing to do to achieve success?
◆ What am I not willing to do to achieve success?

There is considerable benefit to be gained by asking these questions, rather than waiting until you are in the middle of a challenging dilemma. By quietly contemplating these questions you can establish your answers and know what to do when a problem arises.

6 Going deeper

The final exercise simply extends and develops some of the work you will have done in the previous exercise. The aim is to further integrate trustworthiness into your daily life. The first element is to encourage you to keep observing and learning from role models around you. The second element seeks to establish the links between your core purpose and your moral perspective. Finally, the third element seeks to develop your appreciation of, and use of, the three levels of interacting with others.

(a) Identify people (past and present) that you or others would go that 'extra mile' for.

    (i) How do/did they establish this commitment?

    (ii) How do/did they communicate at all three levels?

(b) Take a look at the work you did on your purpose in chapter four. Are your thoughts, feelings and actions always in line with your purpose?

(c) Get into the habit of noticing the surface, feeling the core three levels of interacting with friends and colleagues.

One of the ways we improve our peace of mind is to develop a moral compass. When we behave with integrity we make it easier for people to trust us. This creates the foundation for better long-term relationships. When these exist you can focus your energy on being creative rather than patching up problems.

08

chapter eight
creativity – catching monkeys and empty car parks

Ever-changing world

I must be getting old. I am certainly getting older. There's little doubt about that. I am continually surprised at the rapid rate of technological change. This struck me when Her Majesty Queen Elizabeth the Queen Mother died. There was a newspaper feature that listed the technological changes that had occurred since her birth. It seemed to me that, bar the discovery of fire and the invention of the wheel, everything has been invented in the last hundred years.

Now I know that is not strictly true – but it feels that way. Recently I explained to my 11-year-old daughter, Natasha, that I did not have computers at school and as a teenager I played records. She looked at me as if I were a museum piece. There is continuous change and with it comes the need to make personal changes. Standing still is not really an option.

With change comes challenges, risks, potential disasters and triumphs. It is how we respond that is important. Our capacity for creative thought will prove to be critical.

Waves of change

Leading futurist and human potential thinker Dudley Lynch has identified 'waves of change'. These waves incorporate huge cultural, social, economic and technological elements. They determine the environment that we find ourselves in. The earlier 'waves' lasted for long periods of time. The later ones have a shorter duration but a huge impact.

Wave 1

This was the domain of the farmer and was dominated by agricultural activities. This wave lasted almost six thousand years. The work activities and social bonds hardly changed at all. Many generations came and went. Each would easily recognize the lifestyles of those who came many years before or later. Here humans had 'all the time in the world' to change.

Wave 2

The industrial revolutions and the industrial era saw the pace pick up considerably. There were new ways of working, living and socializing. Whole new industries and business sectors emerged. These industries did not stay still. Suddenly people were expected to make changes far more quickly.

Wave 3

The industrial age has been superseded by the information wave. This has been ushered in by the revolution in computer hardware and software. Once again, new industries have emerged. There is a greater emphasis on 'weightless' products and 'intelligence workers'. This wave has only been in existence for 25 years or so. We have seen old, established skills like printing give way to emerging information technology skills. The rate of change in the information age is staggering. Today's laptop on a school pupil's desk carries more power than a laboratory full of machines from the early 1970s.

For people living through Wave 3 and beyond there will be many changes, challenges and ructions within their individual lifetimes.

Wave 4 and beyond?

Dudley Lynch suggests that Wave 3 is already starting to make way for Wave 4. In this latest wave there is artificial intelligence, biotechnology, robotics and nanotechnology.

Lynch observes:

'Because of the acceleration of the information curve, it can be expected that new waves of change in the near future, and for an indeterminate time thereafter, will arrive virtually 'on the toes' of the previous wave.'

Strategy of the Dolphin by D. Lynch and P. Kordis

If we do not change ourselves during these waves of change we are likely to suffer and be unfulfilled. There is an alternative. That is to adapt and to create our own ways of living! The emotionally intelligent individual will be well placed to manage these changes. One quality that will allow you to thrive is the ability to be creative and innovative.

What is creativity?

For something to be creative there needs to be some form of novelty. If the idea or action is almost identical to something that already exists then it cannot be deemed creative. It is possible to take an established idea or action and place it in a new context. Here the use of a new context is the novel part of the creative process. A good example of this would be Amazon.com. The selling of books is an old, established business. The internet was a new way of transferring information. By combining these two activities Amazon was able to do something novel; something creative.

If a response is to be thought of as creative then it needs to fulfil two criteria; novelty and effectiveness.

A second important aspect of creativity is effectiveness. It is possible to generate dozens, even hundreds, of ideas and actions. Yet all of these potentially creative outputs could be weird and bizarre. They could have the 'virtue' of strangeness yet be unable to deliver any benefits. Often the first stage of finding effective ideas is to generate many weird and wonderful options. However, the test is to find those options that work. One of the difficulties when assessing effectiveness is that some 'potentially' creative approaches can only be evaluated in the long term. When Betamax and VHS videos were developed both were new and 'creative' ideas. Both were novel developments in the world of electronics. Yet, with hindsight and using the criteria of effectiveness, it is obvious that VHS video proved to be genuinely creative.

One further way of differentiating between different types of creativity can be added to these two criteria. You may differentiate between everyday creativity and significant creativity. The everyday variety focuses upon the personal benefits that arise from new ideas and behaviours. To some extent, at an individual level, all learning and development is a creative act as the person applies new ways of thinking and being to their life.

The significant creativity occurs when the creative output has a positive impact on a wider scale. This may be a scientific breakthrough. It may be a new way of doing something in the workplace or an invention.

Innovation and adaptability

In his book *Working with Emotional Intelligence*, Daniel Goleman differentiates between two forms of creative outputs. Each conforms to the criteria for creativity described above. Goleman differentiates between adaptability and innovation.

Innovation

People with this competence:

- seek out fresh ideas from a wide variety of sources
- entertain original solutions to problems / challenges
- produce many new ideas
- take fresh perspectives and risks.

Adaptability

People with this competence:

- smoothly handle multiple demands and changes in priorities

- ◆ amend responses / tactics to fit final changes
- ◆ are flexible on how they see things.

These two approaches can be seen in business. There are the innovative breakthroughs that create whole new industries or transform an industry. The emergence of the information technology industries during the last 20 years have had an impact on every kind of business operation. Even in a traditional business sector like vacuum cleaners the creation of the 'Dyson' machine has turned the sector on its head.

The adaptation approach has been most readily observed in the concept of total quality management. Here business processes are continuously improved. Using a variety of tools, all the employees in an organization attempt to make small incremental improvements. The accumulated impact of many thousands of adaptations leads to huge productivity improvements. It is this accumulation of adaptations that contributed to the Japanese economic miracle.

We see below how the Swiss watch industry failed to innovate. By sticking to old habits we risk the fate of monkeys in Borneo – which I suspect you knew all along. No? Then read on.

Case study

For decades the Swiss watch industry dominated the world marketplace. If you wanted a high quality watch then it would more than likely be Swiss. There was an ongoing process of continuing improvement. The Swiss had invented the minute and second hands on watches. They constantly found new ways to manufacture better gears, cogs, springs, etc. By 1968 this small European country had 65 per cent of the world market and 80 per cent of the profits. By 1980 the market share had dropped to 10 per cent (the luxury end of the market) and the share of profits was down to 20 per cent. How could a market leader for 60 years, committed to improvement and employing well educated people, fall from grace?

The answer is remarkably simple. The Swiss watch industry continued to focus upon mechanical watches when an alternative – electronic quartz – became available. The Swiss watch industry believed it would not appeal to the public. They were wrong. Between 1979 and 1981 the numbers employed in the Swiss watch industry fell from 62,000 to 12,000. What makes this dramatic change even more surprising is that the ability to have electronic quartz movement on timepieces was developed at the research institute in Neufchatel – in SWITZERLAND!

Catching monkeys

In Borneo tribesmen have learned that monkeys will not let go of a nut once they have one in their hand. With this in mind, the tribesmen hollow out coconut shells and leave a small hole in them. They place a nut inside the shell. A length of string is tied to the coconut and the hunters then hide.

The monkeys come along, see the nut, put their hand in the shell and grasp the nut. When the monkeys take hold of the nut their hand becomes a fist. The hole in the coconut is large enough for a flat hand to get into. However, the hole is too small for a fist to be removed from it. The monkey will not let go of the nut, so their fist remains stuck in the coconut.

Gradually, the hunters pull the coconut towards themselves. The monkey does not let go and it gets caught. It is the unwillingness to change behaviour that leads to the capture of the monkey.

Likewise, in life there is a tendency to hold on to fixed ways of thinking and behaving. This may be acceptable when you want a predictable outcome in a predictable environment. However, this option does not apply when the person themselves wishes to change or the environment changes. In these circumstances there is a need for the ability to create new ways of being. By definition, this will require us to break out of some familiar thinking patterns. These patterns may have been established and applied when it was sensible to do so. As times change the patterns may need to change too.

Empty car parks

'If you always do what you've always done, you'll always get what you've always got.'

Anon

I remember once entering a very large, empty car park. At the far end of the car park was the entrance to the building that I was visiting. The car park had white lines neatly marking out the parking spaces.

As the car park was empty, I drove the shortest route to a convenient parking slot. I drove diagonally across many empty slots. The car that followed me into the car park carefully drove along the 'road' and never cut across the white lines, finally parking very close to my car. I received a withering look from the driver – as If I'd insulted his favourite daughter.

There is no 'right or wrong' here. There is difference. Is your life typified by never crossing the 'white lines'? Could you benefit from challenging rules? To be creative means crossing those lines – are you willing to do it?

To be creative means crossing those lines – are you willing to do it?

Two models of creativity

Now I give you not one, but two models of creativity. Not only that, but they are not mutually exclusive. They are complementary. The first was developed by an eminent scientist. It has been tried, tested and taught successfully for many years. The second is something I have put together.

Poincaré's four stages

The nineteenth century mathematician Poincaré devised a four stage model of creativity. This is still one of the most widely used methods for understanding creativity.

◆ Stage I: Preparation

Immersing oneself in the problem. The primary activity here is to precisely define the problem. Once this has been done there is the need to gather a broad range of data and information. During this stage there can be frustration as there are many possibilities and few insights.

◆ Stage II: Incubation

The information and possibilities collected in Stage I are now allowed to stay in the subconscious mind. The brain can play with this information. It can make new connections and generate new ideas and possibilities.

◆ Stage III: Illumination

This is the stage of a breakthrough. When an idea/solution comes to mind it is very exhilarating. The illumination is combined with excitement and energy.

◆ Stage IV: Execution

A great idea means little if nothing happens after its inception. The important fourth stage is to mobilize resources and to take action. To make things happen may require considerable persistence. At times there may be setbacks and hitches. By combining creative ideas with determination you are far more likely to get results.

To be creative you need to work through these stages. By having precision in the earliest stage you ensure that your brain knows exactly what is required. The incubation element implies a willingness to trust your subconscious/unconscious processes. It is rarely possible to force yourself to be consciously creative. In the latter case you are using only a small part of your brain's capacity. The willingness to notice the breakthroughs and then act is important for the specific problem you are addressing. However, it has a longer term impact. The brain will be less inclined to come up with new ideas if it knows that no action will be taken.

Morgan's dynamics of creativity

I will now share with you the simple Morgan model of creativity. It will explain some of the dynamics of being creative and innovative. Once you understand the model you will be able to deepen your understanding of it by applying it in your daily life.

Creative tension

You may call your current world – your current lifestyle: CURRENT REALITY. This is your comfort zone. Here you have thoughts, feelings and behaviours that allow you to get through each day reasonably effectively. However, at times you define a new (future) state of affairs that you desire. A systematic approach to defining this future is goal setting. If you already possessed certain things you would not be setting a goal to have them. If you don't have them then you set a goal for the future. This is your FUTURE REALITY.

The gap between your current reality and your desired future reality leads to psychological tension as shown above. It is sometimes called 'cognitive dissonance'. This is an uncomfortable, stressful feeling. Our brain has a powerful motivational driver to minimize these stresses. In this case it needs to reduce the gap between current reality and future reality.

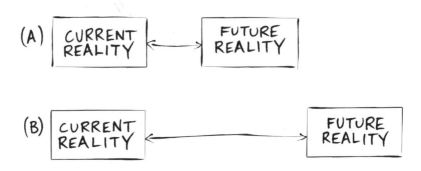

In the above diagram the gap between the current reality (CR) and future reality (FR) is greater in option (b). Here there will be greater dissonance and a greater 'need' to reduce the tension.

At this stage the brain needs to find thoughts, feelings and behaviours that reduce the gap. This is when the brain's creativity is activated. It must come up with ways of closing the CR-FR gap as quickly as possible. Not surprisingly, the brain recognizes that the current reality is based on more concrete experiences while the future reality is 'wishful thinking'. For this reason, a favourite response by the creative part of the brain is to come up with reasons why you should let go of the future and focus upon the current reality.

So when people set challenging goals the brain acknowledges the tension and seeks to reduce it. The creative brain comes up with excuses and rationalizations all aimed at giving up on the future. Here are some typical examples.

'You can't do it.'
'You aren't clever/tough/rich/talented/ enough to do it.'
'People like you don't achieve those sort of things.'
'It will cost you.'
'Don't be big headed/so sure of yourself.'
'It'll end in tears.'
'Why not do X instead?' (X being part of your current reality.)
'You've tried things before and failed.'
'Other people tried this and failed.'

There are hundreds of other examples and variations. All aim to sow the seeds of doubt about the future reality. Once this creeps into thoughts and feelings then doubts appear. The person is tempted to redefine their future reality. In most cases the future reality moves far closer to the current reality.

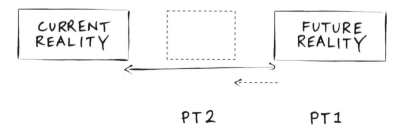

When the future reality is modified it is moved from point 1 to point 2. When this is done the person feels less tension. They feel better in themselves. So they have the evidence of their own feelings: when they amend their goals downwards they feel better. This 'justifies' the change. Also, the creative aspect of the brain reinforces the change with reasons why it was a good idea to do so.

Now consider a different scenario. Here there is the tension of a gap between current and future reality. Only this time the person will NOT let go of the future reality. They keep it fixed in place. The brain initially comes up with all the reasons for quitting that were listed above, plus many, many more. However, the person keeps on focusing upon future reality.

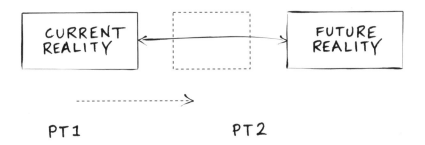

Eventually, the creative part of the brain realizes that the excuses are not working. Yet it must still reduce the tension. In this case it must come up with ways of moving current reality towards future reality. It must generate ideas and actions that close the gap. So the current reality at point 1 is taken closer to point 2.

Once again the closing of the gap results in a reduction of the psychological tension. This causes the person to feel better. Here the good feeling reinforces the brain generating new ideas and behaviours. With practice the brain recognizes that when there is a gap between the current and the future it will be expected to be positively creative to solve the problem.

While this model may be simple, it provides a valuable bridge for some of the issues covered in earlier chapters. First, the importance of goal setting is now abundantly clear. The precise definitions of goals provide a precise definition of future reality. Furthermore, there was considerable emphasis placed upon making sure that your goals are linked to your purpose. When your future reality is built upon your strongest desires you will 'stick with it'. You will not want to compromise it. This supports it and leads to creative impulses that push you towards a desired state rather than pull you back to the old one.

When we take a closer look at emotional management we will see that important elements of this competence include the ability to tolerate the psychological tensions that try and drag you back to the status quo. As you improve your emotional management you are more resilient, persistent and focused. All these qualities enable you to 'hang tough' and allow your constructive creativity to flow.

All these qualities enable you to 'hang tough' and allow your constructive creativity to flow.

The Morgan model can be combined with Poincaré's. The precise definition of the future can be combined with the Preparation stage. As you continue to focus on your goals and affirmations you can allow the Incubation phase to come up with ideas that move you towards your future reality. By acting on your creative ideas (Illumination and Execution) you make progress, reduce tension and realize your goals.

Before looking at some helpful creativity techniques, it is worth touching on how creativity can be killed.

Killing creativity

When you look at the creative process it is worth understanding the ways in which creativity is killed. The Harvard psychologist Teresa Amabile identified four organizational creativity killers. Each killer results in restricting the powers of the memory. They stifle new ideas and the willingness to take risks.

1 Surveillance

This is when senior managers 'hover' and constantly scrutinize what is being done. It results in people feeling they are restricted and not free to think for themselves.

2 Evaluation

This is an overly strong tendency to assess, check and evaluate. Often this is critical and destructive. There is a preoccupation with judgement. This inhibits the willingness to think of something new and to try it out as it is better to stick to the usual way of doing things.

3 Overcontrol

When there is micro-management of every detail then there is a tendency to focus on operational issues. It results in people feeling restricted and disinclined to think originally.

4 Relentless deadlines

When people have huge work pressure they focus only on the job in hand. If the deadlines are relentless then people will not risk anything new nor waste time on it. While stretching goals are motivating and challenging, when it goes too far people are stressed and can be broken.

The Amabile research was ostensibly focused upon organizations. However, the ways that creativity is killed can also be applied to life in general. Sometimes these methods are used within the family. They are often to be found in schools. These creativity killers are imposed on schools by political paymasters who in turn impose them on the children. Indeed, educators may break away from this system so that they can enable their pupils to tap into their creativity. Finally, there are some societies and cultures that encourage creativity while others appear to be designed to squeeze it out of people.

The important thing when managing yourself is to take responsibility for your own creativity.

The important thing when managing yourself is to take responsibility for your own creativity. You must accept that there will often be parameters and constraints. Whatever these may be you can still begin the creative process. In the exercises that follow you will be given proven techniques that will enable you to be more creative.

Activities

To improve the quality of your life may require you to do new things in new ways. These changes become easier if you are creative. The activities below will help you to make improvements. Start by completing your self-rating scale. The lower your score the more you need to work through the activities. As you use these techniques again and again you will be able to be creative automatically.

1 Where are you now? Self-rating

Score yourself on the scale from 1 to 10 for each statement.

10 = Total agreement
1 = Total disagreement

INNOVATION AND CREATIVITY	SCORE
◆ I am rarely comfortable doing the same things the same way.	_____
◆ I regularly think of innovative projects.	_____
◆ I am good at generating new ideas.	
◆ I can easily adapt my thinking and the way I do things.	_____
◆ I am excited by new ideas.	_____
◆ I am willing to try out new products and services.	_____
◆ I often come up with new and useful solutions.	_____
◆ I regularly have flashes of inspiration.	_____
TOTAL	

2 Habit breakers

So much of our life is set in habitual routines. If you observe yourself or other people you will see this is true. We like to read certain newspapers, put on our clothes in a certain order, take preferred routes to our destinations and work in certain ways. Often these may be very efficient. We can do them with little effort. However, sometimes better alternatives exist. The challenge is to check out our habits and keep the ones that work and change the ones that do not work.

Begin by noticing your habits/routines at home and work. For each, list at least two alternatives. Is it possible that the alternatives would lead to a better quality of life, even on a small issue?

This activity encourages you to become an options thinker as well as generating specific options.

Some activities where you could consider alternatives include:

◆ your route to work
◆ how you dress
◆ what foods you eat
◆ the time you spend watching TV
◆ your career.

By getting into the habit of increasing your self-awareness, considering alternatives and taking action, you train your brain to do this automatically.

3 Scamper technique

When you are trying to come up with new ideas, it is sometimes difficult to spontaneously come up with options. This next technique provides a quick and easy way to come up with new possibilities. This technique was developed by Michael Michalko, author of *Thinkertoys*, a groundbreaking book on business creativity. It uses a series of questions devised around the acronym SCAMPER.

- First identify the subject you want to think about.
- Ask the SCAMPER questions about elements of the problem/challenge you face. Make a note of any ideas that emerge.

  S = Substitute?
  C = Combine?
  A = Adapt?
  M = Modify?/Magnify?
  P = Put to other uses?
  E = Eliminate? (Minimize?)
  R = Reverse?/Rearrange?

- Begin by using the technique on small day-to-day problems. Then move on to bigger issues.
- Below are examples of the application of the techniques.

  S = In sport a coach may substitute one player for another.
  C = The creation of a single bank account covering mortgages, loans, savings, etc.
  A = Bookstores developing online capability to sell their products.
  M = Making changes in the route taken to work or the way you do a job.
  P = The technologies of space travel were used for domestic purposes.
  E = Many companies have eliminated retailers and sold directly to the public.
  R = Choosing to become proactive rather than reactive.

With a little practice you will find yourself automatically using the whole range of SCAMPER questions, or at least a few of them. They provide a useful 'icebreaker' for creative thinking. The next technique is another nice example of an 'icebreaker'.

4 Stand on its head

There are some simple ways of loosening things up and encouraging creativity. One is to challenge assumptions. Sometimes the assumptions we hold are the barriers to us finding solutions.

Take a few minutes and apply the following technique to an issue in your life. By doing so you challenge the status quo. If your current approach withstands the detailed scrutiny you may be confident that it has some validity. If it is undermined then it may be time to do something else.

(a) Clearly state your challenge or problem.

(b) Make a list of your assumptions.

(c) Be willing to challenge your most valued and fundamental assumptions.

(d) Stand each assumption on its head (reverse it). Write down the opposite of each assumption.

(e) Carefully note any viewpoints that might prove useful.

(f) Make notes on how each reversal would be operationalized.

---

5 Secret agent

In the USA the Central Intelligence Agency wanted to encourage its agents to approach a challenge from several perspectives. To do this it devised the Phoenix Checklist. Whenever you have a challenge, be willing to use the checklist. With time, and practice, you can add to/subtract from the checklist. This is what you need to do:

(a) Clearly state your challenge or problem.

(b) Apply the checklist to the problem.

(c) Carefully make notes on your answers.

(d) Are any actions to be taken? Create a plan.

(e) Apply the checklist to the plan.

The problem

◆ Why do you need to solve the problem?

◆ What benefits will you receive by solving the problem?

◆ What is not known?

◆ What is it you don't currently understand?

◆ What information is currently available?

◆ What isn't the problem?

◆ Is the information sufficient? Or is it insufficient? Or contradictory?

◆ Should you draw a diagram of the problem?

◆ Where are the boundaries of the problem?

◆ Can you separate and sub-divide the various parts of the problem? What are the relationships of the parts of the problem?

◆ What are the unchangeable elements of the problem?

◆ Have you seen this problem before – or something like it?

◆ Do you know a related problem?

◆ If you find a problem related to yours that has already been solved can you use the solution yourself?

◆ Can you restate or reframe your problem? How many different ways can you do it?

◆ What are the best, worst and most probable cases you can imagine?

The plan

◆ Can you solve the whole, or part, of the problem?

◆ What would you see as an ideal outcome?

◆ How much of the unknown can you determine?

◆ Are you able to conclude something useful from the information you have?

- Have you used all the information that is available?
- Can you clearly define the steps in the problem solving process? Can you be confident of the correctness of each step?
- How many creative thinking techniques can you use to generate ideas?
- How many different kinds of outcomes can you see?
- How many different ways have you tried to solve the problem?
- What have other people done?
- What does your intuition tell you?
- What should be done?
- How / When / Where should it be done?
- Who should do it?
- What do you need now?
- Who will be responsible for what activities?
- What is the unique set of qualities that makes this problem what it is compared with any other?
- What milestones can be used to mark your progress?
- How will you know when you are successful?

The value of this approach is due to the extensive list of questions. It is also equally split between being creative to come up with solutions AND creatively operating the plan. One of the recurring themes in creativity and innovation is that bright ideas in themselves are not enough. There is a need to combine them with action.

6 Wise council

A great way to come up with new solutions and plans is to wonder how great thinkers and doers might respond to your challenge. The Wise Council technique provides an excellent format for tapping into the creativity of others.

(a) Create your personal Wise Council. Select those people, living or dead, real or fictional, who appeal to you for one reason or another. Be sure to select the people you wish to use. Popular examples include:

Albert Schweitzer	John F. Kennedy	Sherlock Holmes
Aldous Huxley	Julius Caesar	Sigmund Freud
Aristotle	Leonardo Da Vinci	Stephen Hawkings
Charles Dickens	Margaret Thatcher	Steven Spielberg
Diogenes	Nelson Mandela	Sun Tzu
Eugene O'Neill	Peter the Great	Thomas Jefferson
George Patton	Plato	Toni Morrison
Gladstone	Ralph Waldo Emerson	W. Somerset Maugham
Isaac Newton	Rupert Murdoch	William Shakespeare
Jesus Christ	Seamus Heaney	Winston Churchill

(b) When you have a challenge, imagine that you are consulting your Wise Council. Select an adviser and choose a favourite quotation by that person.

(c) Reflect on the quotation. Write down your thoughts, regardless of their appropriateness to the challenge. If you think something, write it down, and try to use your thoughts to generate more relevant thoughts. The basic rules are:
- first focus on quantity
- defer judgement
- freewheel
- seek to combine and improve your thoughts.

(d) When you are ready choose the thought, or combination of thoughts, that offers the most promise. Then restate it.

(e) Give yourself a few minutes to come up with further new ideas. If you produce nothing significant, select another quote or go to another adviser. Keep consulting your Wise Council until a quote or passage provokes usable ideas.

The important issue here is not to get bogged down with any one person. You should allow the wise people to spark spontaneous ideas. If one does not help then try another until you get something worthwhile.

---

7 Edward de Bono's six thinking hats

One of the most creative thinkers on creative thinking is Edward de Bono. His many books, articles and seminars provide a wealth of ideas for anyone interested in creativity. One of his most elegant approaches is his six thinking hats technique.

The purpose here is to encourage you to get out of your habitual way of thinking and to view situations from several viewpoints. This allows you to take many points of view into account. As you read the descriptions of the different 'hats' (ways of thinking), ask yourself which one you use most often. You can sit in different places or even wear different-coloured hats to accentuate the different thinking modes.

White hat – cool and neutral

Here you are objective and collect data. Relevant questions are:

◆ What data do we have?
◆ What data is still needed?
◆ Where can we find the data?

No evaluations are passed in white hat mode.

Red hat – fiery and hot

Here you'll be involved with feelings, intuition, hunches and emotions. Typical red hat statements are:

◆ My hunch is . . .
◆ My gut says . . .
◆ My intuition leads me to expect that . . .

Intuition is important because it is the accumulation of our experience and knowledge processed unconsciously.

Black hat – cautious and critical

Here thinking is critical and cautious. It prevents us acting impulsively. Black hats always see the difficulties in situations, not the solutions. Black hats say:

◆ 'That's against the law.'
◆ 'We tried that years ago, it didn't work then and it won't work now.'
◆ 'We can't possibly meet those deadlines.'

Black hat thinking is a useful foil to other modes of thinking. Don't use it too often or you'll demotivate people and stifle innovation.

Yellow hat – sunny and cheerful

This mode is optimistic and pragmatic. You will be focused positively on solutions rather than problems. In this mode you'll be saying things like:

◆ 'That's a top idea, though it will take longer than you've allowed.'
◆ 'The company would get real benefits from that move.'
◆ 'There may be problems but let's try it for a week and then do a review.'

We all need some yellow hat thinking to encourage creativity and flexibility.

Green hat – luxuriant and creative

The green hat is really creative, generating a range of alternative ways of approaching situations. Green hats enjoy looking at possibilities. They say things like:

◆ 'Hey, I can think of half a dozen ways that might work.'
◆ 'What other ideas does anyone have?'
◆ 'How else can we solve the problem?'

Green hats enjoy making creative suggestions. They encourage others to do the same.

Blue hat – helicopter mind/overview

Here you take an overview of situations and think through the processes involved in a logical way. Blue hats establish the boundaries of the subject under discussion. They use chairing skills of summarizing, reaching conclusions and making decisions. Blue hats say things like:

◆ 'Let's have some green hat thinking on this topic.'
◆ 'Could you summarize the points you've been making?'
◆ 'Let's take a break and look at this from a black hat perspective.'

Blue hats are useful for chairing meetings, assessing priorities and recognizing constraints.

By understanding how the creative process works and having the techniques described above at your disposal, you will be able to improve your creativity. As with all the techniques in the book, you will make discernible progress if you apply what you have learned and persevere.

09

chapter nine
emotional management –
marshmallows and
mental toughness

Holyfield's ear

Daniel Goleman provides an excellent example of poor emotional
control when he describes the fight between Mike Tyson and
Evander Holyfield. In their 1997 world title fight we saw a classical
case of amygdala hijacking. It led to Holyfield losing a bit of his ear
and cost Mike Tyson $3 million as well as a one year ban from
boxing.

Early in the fight, Mike Tyson 'lost it'. He stopped boxing and got in
very close on Holyfield. He then bit off a part of his ear. To
understand this brutal and self-destructive behaviour we need to
understand what goes on in our brains at times of stress.

We all have an evolutionarily older part of the brain called the limbic
system. The structure within this that has a key role in emotional
emergencies is called the amygdala. You can think of the amygdala
as the brain's emotional memory bank. Here all our highs and lows
are stored. With all this information carefully stored, the brain can
then scan all incoming information. This information is compared
with our earlier experiences. In this way the brain is able to detect
the appropriate response.

In an earlier fight, Holyfield had 'head butted' Tyson. This led to
Tyson complaining when he lost the fight. The 'head butting'
happened again in the second fight. The amygdala is wired to give
an instantaneous response. There is no reflection or pause for
thought. The brain responds to this crisis in a predictable way with
heightened sensory awareness, the closing down of complex thought
and knee jerk responses. In the fight this led to Tyson going berserk

and biting his opponent. He lost the fight and all his professional credibility.

One team that did not succumb to an amygdala hijacking was Manchester United in the 1999 European cup final. They were losing 1–0 with just over a minute of the game remaining. In such circumstances, it would be easy for individual players and the team as a whole to capitulate. However, Manchester United kept going. They played their usual game and persisted. They maintained their skill levels as time ran down. The result was a 2–1 victory as United scored two goals in a minute. The German opposition was devastated.

Case study

England and Manchester United football star David Beckham is an excellent emotional management case study.

In 1998 he was sent off in a World Cup knock-out game between England and Argentina. After being fouled, he petulantly kicked the guilty player. A foolish emotional response undermined the chances of the whole team. England eventually lost the game.

The domestic football season in 1999 put Beckham under extreme pressure. He was reviled by many supporters. They resented his superstar lifestyle, his marriage to a pop star and his sending off in the World Cup. In every game thousands of people hoped to see him fail, while others demanded success. When games were televised the thousands became millions. Opponents sought to close him down by fair means or foul. The press were 'on Beckham's back'. Also, at many games a section of the opposition's fans would chant disgusting things about Beckham and his wife.

Yet Beckham had a magnificent season. He played to a world class standard week in and week out. He did not make excuses or plead for sympathy. He simply showed his mental toughness and resilience.

The reasons our brain can cope with stressful situations is because of the capabilities of another part of the brain. The prefrontal lobes take the raw impulses and 'filter' them. These lobes have at their disposal the rules of life and greater clarity on the most skilful ways to respond to a situation. There is a tension between the amygdala and the prefrontal lobes. Will a person just jump in or will they consider their actions carefully? At times the knee jerk reflex response may lead to disaster. Likewise, a person in a dangerous situation may need to act quickly rather than take time to make a decision. The challenge is to get the right balance.

The challenge is to get the right balance.

In sport self-control can be the difference between world class success and abject failure. The technical skills or fitness of the athletes are not in question. The ability to manage emotions can be critical. This is true for every other walk of life. Are people able to perform well under pressure? It is possible for people to have a high level of skill yet they cannot perform under pressure. Some people are able to bounce back after setbacks while others do not. Here it is characteristics like persistence and resilience that make the difference.

Why two marshmallows are good for you

Picture the scene. It is 1968 and researchers at Stanford University have just conducted an experiment called the 'marshmallow test'. They worked with pre-school four year olds. Each child was brought into a room. A marshmallow was put on a table in front of them. They were told that they could eat the marshmallow immediately. However, if they waited for the researcher to return from an errand they would be given a second marshmallow.

The aim was to explore how young children manage their impulses. Would they be able to delay the gratification of eating a marshmallow straight away? The Stanford researchers found that some children ate the marshmallow straight away. Others struggled to hold off but failed. In the third group were children who found ways to resist eating the marshmallow. They did things such as cover their eyes, sing songs and play games.

The children were revisited 14 years later as they left senior school. The children who ate the marshmallow straight away were compared with those who waited and got two. The one marshmallow eaters were again found to be more likely to crack under pressure, had temper problems, were more likely to be tempted off course, were less socially competent and were also unwilling to take risks.

Perhaps even more surprising was the discovery that the two marshmallow children were far superior as students compared with the one marshmallow group. This came from reports given by the parents. It also came from SAT test scores. The one marshmallow students had an average score of 1052, while the two marshmallow students got 1262. A difference of 210. Indeed, this 1 v. 2 marshmallow test was a better predictor of academic performance than IQ tests with the four year olds.

Once again the research done over decades shows that emotional intelligence has a significant impact on the quality of our lives.

Getting mentally tough

'How does a track star like Gail Devers, critically ill and within a breath of having both legs amputated, return to health to claim the title of the world's fastest woman alive? Their secret lies inside. A refusal to give up. A resilience. A certain perspective. Mental toughness.'

Alan Goldberg, sports psychologist

For many years it had been recognized that some people were more resilient than others. Those people who were mentally tough seemed to get far better results than others. Initially, it was believed that you were either born with mental toughness or you were not. However, we now know that mental toughness is determined by your explanatory style. Some explanatory styles make you tougher than others. The good news is that if your current style is not producing good results you can change it.

Explanatory styles

According to Martin Seligman, the eminent psychologist, your explanatory style is the habitual way that you explain good and bad events to yourself. This is more than the words you use to describe a situation. It is your deeper habit of thinking and feeling. This habit is learned in childhood and adolescence.

Seligman found that your explanatory style has a significant impact on your ultimate success or failure in life. This is because your explanatory style influences your motivation and ability to persist.

The explanatory style can be divided into three components: permanence, pervasiveness, and personalization. The way these are used at times of adversity or success will indicate whether a person is defined as optimistic or pessimistic.

1 *Permanence*

Here the issue is how do people respond to setbacks. Do they believe a setback is a temporary blip or a permanent part of their lives? Conversely, when things go well do people think it is temporary or permanent?

2 *Pervasiveness*

Here the issue is the degree to which a setback is treated as an isolated event or is it put in a wider context of failure? For example, a driver takes three or four attempts to complete a reverse parking manoeuvre. It is possible to just think it was a localized problem. However, it could be seen as an example of being a bad driver, having poor co-ordination or being a general failure.

3 *Personalization*

The third aspect of explanatory styles refers to the tendency to blame yourself (internal) or other causes (external) when events go badly. This is not an issue of taking responsibility. With blame it is a destructive and emotionally negative response.

Optimism and pessimism

The emotional management quality that focuses upon optimism and pessimism has been extensively researched. The results follow a consistent pattern and show that in all areas that contributed to a better quality of life it is better to be optimistic.

In a five year study of insurance sales staff it was shown that people with a more optimistic explanatory style sold substantially more policies and stayed in their jobs longer than pessimists. The optimistic sales people outsold pessimists by 88 per cent. The pessimists were three times more likely to quit. Furthermore, a two year study of estate agents showed that optimistic staff outsold pessimists by between 250 per cent and 320 per cent.

There is also considerable evidence that optimists are healthier than pessimists.

There is also considerable evidence that optimists are healthier than pessimists. In an innovative study that covered 52 years, Seligman found that optimists lived longer than pessimists. There are also indications that people of an optimistic disposition have stronger immune systems.

Case study

An excellent example of optimism in sport is the story of Olympic swimmer Matt Biondi. He was hailed as a superstar in the run up to the 1988 Olympics. He was compared favourably with the greatest Olympic swimmer ever, Mark Spitz.

At the Olympics Biondi finished third in his first event. Then in his second event he was inched out of the gold medal at the end of the race. This led to widespread speculation that Biondi's efforts would end in abject failure such as he would either fail to get a gold medal or quit altogether. However, Biondi bounced back and won five consecutive gold medals. This response came as no surprise to Martin Seligman. He had tested Biondi's explanatory style. He knew Biondi was optimistic. In experiments he found that Biondi would redouble his efforts when he had setbacks.

It is possible to summarize the explanatory styles of optimists and pessimists in adverse and successful situations (see below). The key point to recognize on all this research is actually summarized in the title of Seligman's groundbreaking book: *Learned Optimism*. These styles are learned. They are not genetically hard-wired into our brains. This means it is possible to learn to move from pessimism to optimism.

The explanatory styles of optimists and pessimists	
Pessimists	
Situation	**Response**
Adversity	Permanent
	Pervasive
	Personal
Success	Temporary
	Limited
	External
Optimists	
Situation	**Response**
Adversity	Temporary
	Limited
	External
Success	Permanent
	Pervasive
	Personal

Take a quick look at the explanatory styles in the tables above. Which ones most closely describe your own responses? You will be exploring your styles later in the chapter. Even if you are a pessimist, do not worry (though at the moment worry is your style!), change is possible. Seligman and his colleagues have done extensive work teaching people to think optimistically. For example, they have worked with highly pessimistic school children. By giving them regular lessons on different explanatory styles it was possible to bring about lasting improvements. The children were happier, attended school more regularly and performed better academically. In the activities later in the chapter you will learn how to change your explanatory styles.

Please release me

When unsuitable or unpleasant emotions arise, they are likely to adversely affect the quality of our lives. They cause us to feel bad. They may well weaken us physically and leave us susceptible to illness. They will often impair our decision making and responses. When unwanted emotions occur there are three common responses – suppress, express or exit.

In many situations a person may have a strong emotional reaction. One way they try and deal with it is via suppression. They attempt to push the feeling deeper inside themselves. There is a tendency to deny the feelings. An additional approach to suppression is to deaden the pain by using alcohol or drugs. While suppression may lead to some temporary relief, it may leave the underlying issues unchanged. This means the emotions are likely to re-emerge and require further suppression.

A second response to unwanted emotions takes an opposite approach to suppression. In this case there is an emotional outpouring. This is, more often than not, seen in manifestations of anger, aggression, tantrums and sulking. Here the person is expressing their feelings. While people try to justify 'letting off steam', it usually ruins relationships and causes problems. The idea of it being 'better out than in' may provide the person with temporary relief. However, in most cases these outbursts repeat themselves. The expression does not lead to a permanent resolution. Furthermore, the expression of emotions often poisons relationships on a long-term basis.

A third and final common response is called Exit. When situations lead to destructive emotions, people may suppress or express them.

To avoid this happening, some people choose to get away from the difficult situation. They may run away or leave the room or whatever it takes. There is also a tendency to avoid the situations where such emotions may arise. At times this is a sensible response. However, if you avoid places that are important to your life then it can become problematic.

While we tend to use the SEE model (see below), the outcomes are rarely fully adequate. So sometimes we try one method and if it does not work we redouble our efforts. Typical examples are drinking even more to deaden feelings or having even bigger emotional outbursts. Alternatively, people try one approach and then swing across and try another.

THE SEE MODEL

S = SUPPRESS

E = EXPRESS

E = EXIT

Fortunately, there is an alternative that works wonderfully for destructive emotions. This approach is called 'letting go' or 'releasing'. There are several exponents of this approach. One of the most eminent is Dr Patricia Carrington, former lecturer at Princeton University. In her work as a clinical psychologist she recognized that people using the SEE model suffered from stress related illnesses, family relationship problems and depression.

The release approach encourages people to just 'let go' of a feeling.

The release approach encourages people to just 'let go' of a feeling. Instead of trying to do something with a feeling, the alternative is to allow the emotion to 'float away'. Like the young monk in the story below, there is a tendency to hold on to emotions that harm us.

Case study

A Zen tale tells of two pious monks who were on their yearly pilgrimage through the mountains when they caught sight of a young woman by the edge of a brook. She had fallen from her horse and injured her foot. In the meantime her animal had wandered off, crossed the brook by itself and stood grazing indifferently on the far bank.

Spying the two monks, the young woman hastily signalled to them and begged them to carry her across the stream, which she could not cross alone because of her injury. She was anxious to remount her horse and ride to safety before dark.

Despite the young woman's pleas the younger of the two monks declined to assist her because of his vow of chastity, which forbade him ever touching a woman. The elder monk reacted differently. Realizing how few travellers ever went that way and aware of the dangers that might beset the young woman at nightfall, he swiftly carried her across the brook, placed her on her horse and made sure that she started safely on her journey home.

The two monks then resumed their pilgrimage. When they had travelled down the road a short way, the younger one, becoming more upset each moment by what he had seen, was finally unable to contain himself any longer and cried out to his companion, 'I cannot believe what I saw! You broke your vow of chastity by carrying a woman in your arms!'

The elder monk turned to him and with a quiet smile replied, 'But, little brother, I let go of her 10 miles back!'

From *The Power of Letting Go* by Dr P. Carrington

Once you have become aware of your emotions and feelings it is possible to determine whether they are constructive or destructive. In the latter case you now have the option of letting go of that emotion.

If it should return you will also be able to release it again. With time the process of releasing emotions can be done in seconds. It is time to take control and manage your emotions.

Now let's explore some of the ways that you can permanently improve your emotional management and develop the high performance thinking patterns of successful people.

Activities

The activities described below will help you to manage your emotions more effectively. First work through the self-rating scales below. The lower your score the more you need to work on your emotional intelligence.

---

1 Where are you now? Self-rating

Score yourself on the scale from 1 to 10 for each statement.

10 = Total agreement
1 = Total disagreement

EMOTIONAL MANAGEMENT   **SCORE**

- ◆ I bounce back after a setback. _____
- ◆ I can put off fun tasks to do what needs to be done. _____
- ◆ I can stay calm when things hot up. _____
- ◆ I don't need instant gratification. _____
- ◆ I feel in control of my life. _____
- ◆ When I'm in a bad mood I can get myself out of it. _____
- ◆ I can focus on the task in stressful situations. _____
- ◆ I am not easily provoked. _____

TOTAL

2 Delay gratification

Earlier in the chapter we took a look at the marshmallow experiment. It is obvious that the ability to curb our impulses and delay gratification can significantly improve the quality of our lives. To make improvements in this area you need to become mindful of your patterns of impulse control. Then, if necessary, you can take action.

(a) Think about your own impulses. Make a list of those things you like doing that you ought to delay at times. Also make a list of those things you should do that you are inclined to put off.

(b) Once you have written your lists, reflect upon your reasons for these patterns of behaviour.

(c) What would happen in your life if you started doing things that you put off and delaying some things that ought to be delayed?

(d) For one thing that you are delaying, list all the reasons for taking action and then make a commitment to take that action.

3 Managing your emotions

To manage your emotions you must combine two important elements of emotional intelligence. First you need to have an awareness of your emotions and what triggers them. Once this has been done, you can begin to take alternative actions where it is needed.

For each of the emotions in the table below complete each column. Here are some pointers to help you do this.

◆ In column two briefly note how you experience that emotion – ask yourself what physical sensations do you experience? Where in your body do you feel them? How is your breathing/thinking affected?

- In the third column describe the events that trigger the emotion.
- In the last column for negative emotions, describe an alternative response you could have to the triggers – ones that would be more fun and more beneficial.

Emotion	Experience	Triggers	Alternatives
Rage			
Disappointment			
Sadness			
Anxiety			
Joy			
Fear			
Trust			
Amazement			
Guilt			

As you start to recognize the triggers you can use the detachment and pattern breaking techniques described in the exercises below and then try an alternative response.

With practice the alternative response becomes automatic – and also the preferred response.

4 Detachment

A feeling of detachment and distancing of yourself from unpleasant feelings is an excellent way of combating external stress or dealing with negative emotions. This technique enables you to manage strong emotions.

(a) The first way of detaching is as follows:
   (i) Think of a time when you were stressed or had a strong negative experience.
   (ii) Imagine stepping out of your body leaving behind all those responses.

(iii) As you do this be aware of how you become calmer, cooler and more rational compared with how you were when you started.

Having done points (i)–(iii) for a minute or two, return to point (i). Notice how you can keep a sense of detachment while returning to this point.

(b) A second method for dealing with problems is to repeat the following phrases regularly:

'I have behaviours but I am more than those behaviours.'
'I have emotions but I am more than those emotions.'
'I have thoughts but I am more than those thoughts.'
'I am greater than those behaviours, feelings and thoughts.'

By doing detachment exercises you will find that you are more able to detach yourself from destructive emotions or feelings.

(c) A further variation of the detachment technique is to work through examples (a) and (b) while maintaining a deep sense of calm and relaxation.

As with all these techniques detachment gets easier and better with practice. Remember you will be working through Quadrant II as you master a new skill. A few minutes a day for several weeks makes the difference. You will then be better able to perform in a balanced way.

5 Pattern breaking

A great way to manage your emotions is to use the pattern break. This is a way of distracting yourself from negative thoughts and feelings. It takes the energy away from them.

The pattern break is a distraction technique. So, once you become aware of a negative feeling you should:

▶

- clap your hands 3–5 times very loudly, or
- slap yourself, or
- shout or say firmly 'NO', or
- have a rubber band on your hand and flick it against your skin, or
- or use any other method that is appropriate to where you are.

Once you have finished the distraction activity, say to yourself, 'That is no longer like me'. You then need to think about something new. Or do something different into which you can channel your energy. When this technique is repeated you soon weaken old problem patterns of thinking and feeling. You undermine problematic habits.

6 Alternative endings

Sometimes film and TV programmes show alternative endings and then one is selected for broadcasting. You can apply this technique to your own life.

In this exercise you contemplate an alternative ending to an established negative feeling, thought or behaviour. Then you select and use an alternative. Have a look through the example below.

Trigger	Feeling	Behaviour
Work pressure	Frustration	Shouting at staff
Work pressure	Patience	Organize work to relieve pressure

- The first line is the negative, while the second is the alternative. Visualise the trigger leading to the alternative response and rehearse it regularly.
- Set a goal for, and affirm the use of, the alternative response.
- When you have done the above regularly, go on to try it out for real at work.

That was the example – now it is your turn to work through the process. If you are like most people, there will be some places in your life that would benefit from this technique. So give it a try.

7 Moving from pessimism to optimism

When you experience the pessimistic thinking identified by Seligman, it is possible to challenge it. By asking questions and giving honest answers, a more constructive mindset can be created. Read through the questions that you can ask at a time of adversity.

Adversity
◆ Will this situation last for the rest of my life?
◆ Can I name another person where this situation lasted for the WHOLE of their life?
◆ Does this situation HAVE to touch EVERY aspect of my life?
◆ Could I name one aspect of my life that is not touched by the adverse situation?
◆ Is every single aspect of this adverse situation due to something in my control?

As you ask these questions, you start to undermine the pessimistic thinking. Likewise, you can challenge the pessimistic response you may have to successes.

Success
◆ Could this positive feeling last five seconds (a minute!) longer than usual?
◆ Could I think about this feeling in a week's time and recall the positive emotion?
◆ Could this positive feeling allow me to feel better when I do something else?
◆ Could this positive feeling have a positive impact on other people?
◆ Is there the slightest/smallest thing that I did that contributed to this success? (Did you turn up? Did you buy a ticket?)

This stuff works. If you feel pessimistic, apply this method. You will feel better. You will be healthier, tougher and happier.

8 The Morgan Release Model

There are many release models. The one that follows offers a simple and effective way to manage limiting emotions in life. The model has three stages. The first stage focuses upon getting precise definitions of the negative feeling, its cause and recognition that alternative emotions are possible. Here is a summary of that first stage.

- Stage 1 (a): Give a precise definition of the emotions. What do you call it? Where do you feel it in your body? How big? What shape? How intense?
- Stage 1 (b): Define the event/situation that triggers the unpleasant emotion.
- Stage 1 (c): Describe 10 alternative positive ways of responding to the trigger.
- Stage 1 (d): Finally, you will ask a few questions, which are detailed later.

Work through stages below. There is an example on page 171 that you can refer to.

Stage 1

(a) Describe the emotion experienced (where in body/shape of feeling/intensity)

(b) Define the event/future event causing the emotion to be experienced

(c) List 10 alternative responses to the trigger

(d) Ask yourself the following questions:

◆ Must the trigger in Stage 1(b) of the Morgan Release Model ALWAYS lead to the emotion in Stage 1(a)?
◆ Are there alternative responses?
◆ Would some alternatives lead to better results?

Stage 2
The emotional response is made up of a cluster of firing brain cells. They can be weakened when emotions are negative. To lessen the hold these emotions have, you can release them. You can let go,

▶

managing yourself

momentum

rather than hold on. Ask yourself the following questions, and answer yes or no.

◆ Is it possible to LET GO of the emotion?
◆ If it is possible, will I LET GO of the emotion?
◆ If it is possible, when will I LET GO of the emotion?

(Do not worry if the answer is no.)

Run through these questions four or five times. After the first couple of run throughs, the questions can be abbreviated to:

◆ Is it possible to let go?
◆ Will I let go?
◆ When will I let go?

The negative emotion should now disappear or diminish rapidly. If it persists, then let go of wanting to change the emotion by amending the questions to:

◆ Can I let go of wanting to change the emotion?
◆ Will I let go of wanting to change the emotion?
◆ When will I let go of wanting to change the emotion?

So, rather than suppress, express or exit, you can 'let go'. This means fears, panics and anxieties can all dissolve.

Stage 3
An alternative or supplement to Stage 2 is emotional balancing. Here a few phrases will once again remove limiting emotions.

◆ Could I allow my body to be as uncomfortable with (NAME FEELING) as it is now?
◆ Could I allow my body to be as comfortable with (NAME FEELING) as it is now?

or

- Could I allow myself to be as unhappy and tense as I am now?
- Could I allow myself to be as happy and relaxed as I am now?

In the balancing examples just repeat one or both pairs several times when addressing a particular problem.

Summarized example

Take a look at the worked example provided here. You will see the release model applied to the fear of failure.

Stage 1

(a) Emotion – fear of failure

(b) Trigger – taking on a senior role

(c) Alternative responses:
Confidence
Rising to the challenge
Happy at promotion
Quitting

(d) Minor discomfort
Indifference
Bemusement
Amusement
Inquisitive about options
Curiosity

Qu. Must the trigger in (b) always lead to the emotion in (a)?
A. No.

Qu. Are there alternative responses?
A. Yes.

Qu. Would some alternatives lead to better performance?
A. Definitely.

Stage 2
- Is it possible to let go of a fear of failure?
- If it is possible, will I let go of a fear of failure?
- If it is possible, when will I let go of a fear of failure?

Abbreviated questions:
- Is it possible to let go?
- Will I let go?
- When will I let go?

Stage 3
- Could I allow my body to be as uncomfortable with a fear of failure as it is now?
- Could I allow my body to be as comfortable with a fear of failure as it is now?

The process gets easier with time. It gets quicker. Indeed, often the problem disappears even before you get to the end of Stage 1.

In competitive situations a difficulty may arise spontaneously. In such cases you can take a short cut to a solution.

- Ask if there are better alternatives.
- Go on to work through Stage 2 or 3 sentences.
- The problem will now be solved.

If you use these emotional management techniques you will reap great rewards. Many of the energy sapping emotions you experience can be negated. You can become far more resilient. Things that would have knocked you off course will not even cause you a second's concern. Furthermore, you will be able to take on more risks and challenges and not be plagued by anxieties and worries.

As you master emotional management, you will become a happier person. This will not be a transient feeling. Instead, you will have a sense of well being day after day. All this is achievable if you apply just a few simple techniques. Do yourself a favour, find half an hour a day for a month. Apply the techniques and transform your life.

chapter ten
just do it!

'Many of life's failures are people who did not realise how close they were to success when they gave up.'

T. Edison

The great news for any person who wants to manage themselves is that they can take any of the different elements of emotional intelligence and improve on it. Furthermore, you can be confident that when your emotional intelligence is elevated, so is the quality of your life. The perplexing question is; why do so few people make these changes?

I have looked for the reason why some people will make the effort to change, while others will not. And why will some people read through this book, accept what is says – and yet do nothing?

The answer to these questions is simple, though it does not offer a magic solution. In the end people make changes because they choose to change and choose to act. Most people do not make these choices. They may be unhappy with their life. They may complain about their life, and even do things to deaden the pain. What they do not do is make the two key choices – to change and to take action.

There are a few people who make a stab at the first area of choice. They want to change. They recognize that life can be better. These people will also make a tentative excursion into the second area of choice. They may try and do something differently, buy a book (like this one) or attend a seminar. However, their commitment to action is tentative. There are many other people who continually do the rounds of the personal development seminars and who read dozens of books, yet push on no further.

Such people are stuck between being unsettled where they are in life and being unable to make the changes they desire. This is not a very nice place to be. At times they will not press on because they hope for instant karma. They keep looking for pain-free, instant change – the wave of a magic wand – that will make everything rosy in the garden. Rather than knuckle down, they prefer to flit from one approach to the next, looking for the instant solution. I wish these people luck. They will need it.

If you think you are similar to those people, then I strongly recommend that your try working through chapter four again. By locking on to your purpose, you may find the energy to become more proactive.

The people who get most out of life choose to change and to take action.

The people who get most out of life choose to change and to take action. They may have an external catalyst that causes them to make these choices. It is also possible to have a series of smaller events that accumulate until new choices are made.

Finally, there are people who can't wait to be proactive. They decide that life can be better and they choose to change and choose to take action. Why they do it is a mystery. But do it – they do!!

I hope you have made similar choices. You have this book so you are at least part of the way there. If you have actively worked through the activities and techniques you already have made considerable progress. If you have not done the activities – then start now! Why not select one chapter and get stuck in? There is no substitute for actually doing it.

The person who manages themselves effectively can master their emotional intelligence. Such a person understands themselves. They have a passionate sense of purpose. They are able to read other people and understand them, and they are trusted by others. The emotionally intelligent person benefits from their intuitive insights and the ability to be creative. They also control their emotions to get the best possible results.

Do you want to live this way? Then just Do It!

momentum prescription – let us help you work out which book will suit your symptoms

Feel stuck in a rut? Something wrong and need help doing something about it?

◆ If you need tools to help making changes in your life: **coach yourself** (a good general guide to change)

◆ If you are considering dramatic career change: **snap, crackle or stop**

◆ If you need to work out what you'd like to be doing and how to get there: **be your own career consultant**

◆ If you need help making things happen and tackling the 'system' at work/in life: **change activist**

◆ If you think you want more from your life than a 'normal' career: **careers un-ltd**

Feel that you can never make decisions and you just let things 'happen'?

◆ If you need help making choices: **the big difference**

◆ If you want to feel empowered and start making things happen for yourself: **change activist**

Feel life is too complicated and overwhelming?

◆ If you need help working through office politics and complexity: **clued up**

◆ If you need a kick up the backside to get out of your commerce-induced coma: **change activist**

◆ If you need an amusing and very helpful modern life survival guide: **innervation**

◆ If you never have enough time or energy to get things done or think properly: **mental space**

Feel like you might be in the wrong job?

◆ If you want help finding your destiny job and inspiration to make that dramatic career change: **snap, crackle or stop**

◆ If you feel like you aren't doing a job that is really 'what you are about': **soultrader**

◆ If you are struggling with the 'do something worthwhile OR make money dilemma': **change activist**

◆ If you think you want more from your life than a 'normal' career: **careers un-ltd**

Feel that you're not the person/leader you should be?

◆ If you want to be the kind of person others want to follow: **lead yourself**

◆ If you don't feel your working relationships with people could improve: **managing yourself**

◆ If you need help becoming the person you've always wanted to be: **reinvent yourself**

◆ If you want to work out everything you've got to offer, and how to improve that: **grow your personal capital**

Feel you need help getting your ideas into action?

◆ If the problem is mainly other people, lack of time and the messiness of life: **clued up**

◆ If the problem is communicating your thinking: **hey you!**

◆ If the problem is getting things across to other people: **managing yourself**

◆ If the problem is more ideas than time and you are a bit overwhelmed with work: **mental space**

◆ If the problem is making change in your life: **coach yourself**

Feel you aren't projecting yourself and managing your career as well as you should?

◆ If you'd like to be the kind of person people think of first: **managing brand me**

◆ If you'd like people to listen to your ideas more readily: **hey you!**

◆ If you'd like to come across as the person you really are inside: **soultrader**

◆ If you need general help in changing the way you work/life: **coach yourself**

◆ If you need help working out what you've got and how best to use it: **float you**

Feel you'd like to be much more creative and a real 'ideas person'.

◆ If you need inspiration on how to be innovative and think creatively: **innervation**

◆ If you need help spreading your ideas and engendering support: **hey you!**

Find Your Purpose – and Make Things Happen

Soultrader

find purpose and you'll find success
Carmel McConnell
1 84304018 2

You're a busy, stressed employee. Your job is probably pretty much ok; maybe better, maybe worse. But whichever, you probably don't have much time or energy to devote to thinking about anything much, outside of coping with workload and what to have for dinner. What difference would it make to your life if you were creating the 'lifelong adventure called my career' based on who you are – at core?

How would you like to feel excited about your life again? Because that's what soultrading is all about. Your soul can help you figure out what you want to be when you grow up. Much more than the boss ever could.

And how would you like to be more successful and high-achieving? Because that's also what soultrading is about – having a personal strategy that you really buy into (and so do others). Discover the 12-day *Soultrader* plan to work out your purpose and develop your personal strategy.

Careers un-ltd

tell me. what is it you plan to do with your one wild and precious life?

Carmel McConnell and Jonathan Robinson
1 84304026 3

You can choose if you want a limited career, or an un-ltd one. This is a very different kind of career book. It's the first ever guide to explore ALL your career options – not just life in big corporates – for anybody who wants more from their career than just a pay packet. It's the rough guide to the world of work.

Featuring the profiles of 10 career pioneers who tell how they created an un-ltd career for themselves, *Careers Un-ltd* will help you think through what you want to do with YOUR 'wild and precious' life.

Available at all good bookshops and online at:
www.business-minds.com   www.yourmomentum.com